Protecting Intellectual Freedom in Your School Library

Intellectual Freedom Front Lines

Protecting Intellectual Freedom in Your Academic Library: Scenarios from the Front Lines,
by Barbara M. Jones

Protecting Intellectual Freedom in Your Public Library: Scenarios from the Front Lines,
by Candace D. Morgan

Protecting Intellectual Freedom in Your School Library: Scenarios from the Front Lines,
by Pat R. Scales

Protecting Intellectual Freedom in Your School Library

Scenarios from the Front Lines

Pat R. Scales

For the Office for Intellectual Freedom

AMERICAN LIBRARY ASSOCIATION

CHICAGO   2009

Sidebars on pp. 2, 7, 11, 18–19, 22–32, 49, 58–59, 62, 72, 75, 84–85, 88, 96–97, 102, and 104 by Deborah Caldwell-Stone. Sidebar on pp. 46–47 by Carrie Russell. Appendix A: Minors' First Amendment Rights to Access Information, by Theresa Chmara, was published in the *Intellectual Freedom Manual,* 7th ed. (Chicago: American Library Association, 2006), 384–93.

The paper used in this publication meets the minimum requirements of American National Standard for Information Sciences—Permanence of Paper for Printed Library Materials, ANSI Z39.48-1992.∞

Library of Congress Cataloging-in-Publication Data
Scales, Pat.
    Protecting intellectual freedom in your school library : scenarios from the front lines / Pat R. Scales for the Office for Intellectual Freedom.
        p. cm. — (Intellectual freedom front lines)
    Includes bibliographical references and index.
    ISBN 978-0-8389-3581-1 (alk. paper)
    1. School libraries—Censorship—United States—Case studies. 2. Intellectual freedom—United States—Handbooks, manuals, etc. I. American Library Association. Office for Intellectual Freedom. II. Title.
Z675.S3S258 2009
025.2'13—dc22
                                                                                        2008039893

ISBN-13: 978-0-8389-3581-1

Printed in the United States of America

13 12 11 10 09   5 4 3 2 1

Contents

Serials Section

Pat R. Scales is a retired middle and high school librarian whose programs have been featured on the *Today Show* and in various professional journals. She received the ALA/Grolier Award in 1997 and was a *Library Journal* Mover and Shaker. She is currently president of the Association of Library Service for Children, a division of the American Library Association. She is the author of *Teaching Banned Books: Twelve Guides for Young Readers* and serves as a spokesperson for first amendment issues as they relate to children and young adults. She writes a bimonthly column for *School Library Journal* and a monthly column for the Random House website, and she is a regular contributor to *Book Links* magazine.

The First Amendment to the U.S. Constitution

Congress shall make no law respecting an establishment of religion, or prohibiting the free exercise thereof; or abridging the freedom of speech, or of the press; or the right of the people peaceably to assemble, and to petition the Government for a redress of grievances.

Library Bill of Rights

The American Library Association affirms that all libraries are forums for information and ideas, and that the following basic policies should guide their services.

I. Books and other library resources should be provided for the interest, information, and enlightenment of all people of the community the library serves. Materials should not be excluded because of the origin, background, or views of those contributing to their creation.

II. Libraries should provide materials and information presenting all points of view on current and historical issues. Materials should not be proscribed or removed because of partisan or doctrinal disapproval.

III. Libraries should challenge censorship in the fulfillment of their responsibility to provide information and enlightenment.

IV. Libraries should cooperate with all persons and groups concerned with resisting abridgment of free expression and free access to ideas.

V. A person's right to use a library should not be denied or abridged because of origin, age, background, or views.

VI. Libraries which make exhibit spaces and meeting rooms available to the public they serve should make such facilities available on an equitable basis, regardless of the beliefs or affiliations of individuals or groups requesting their use.

Adopted June 18, 1948, by the ALA Council; amended February 2, 1961; January 23, 1980; inclusion of "age" reaffirmed January 23, 1996.

Introduction

Real Issues Facing School Library Media Professionals

A school library media coordinator in the state department of education offers support services to elementary, middle, and high school library media specialists in all the school districts in the state. Though there are six or seven urban school districts that have their own school library media coordinators, most of the state's school districts are small and cannot afford support staff to guide their library media specialists in dealing with day-to-day issues. The state's population is quite varied: There are a number of well-established and conservative communities and other more progressive and liberal cities and towns. Some areas are highly industrialized; others are quite rural. Politicians and business leaders are proposing incentives to attract new industry to the state, but at the heart of the matter is the quality of public education. Business and industry are not interested in coming to the state unless schools guarantee a rigorous curriculum and high graduation rates. This is a promise the state can make in the more urban areas, but the rural school districts don't have a large tax base and are very deficient in school rankings. Nevertheless, a few new industries have relocated to the state, causing such overcrowded school conditions in some districts that students cannot possibly reach the level of achievement that is expected.

In recent years, a large number of Hispanic children have enrolled in the schools, requiring school districts to develop classes for English Language Learners (ELL) to better serve this non-English-speaking population. While districts are committed to these children, they are finding it difficult to communicate with their families when very little English is spoken. At the same time, the state is proud of its diversity and offers festivals and celebrations to promote harmony across the state.

Recent growth trends and a concerted effort to improve education for all students have presented some controversies related to libraries. There are parents of gifted children who complain that their children aren't provided enough higher level materials, and others object to materials that are beyond the maturity level of their children. Parents and teachers of students with special needs feel that current school library services don't meet the educational requirements of their children. There are challenges to novels used in the classroom, questions related to computerized reading programs, and issues related to restricted shelves, reserved materials, interlibrary loan, and circulation policies that place economic barriers on many users.

In the past year, there have been questions about labeling students and materials, privacy, Internet use, e-mail accounts, and social networking. All of these issues reflect concerns about library media center access and services to students throughout the state, regardless of how large or small the school or school district.

The state library media coordinator deals with these complaints and offers guidance to school district media coordinators, individual media specialists, principals, and in some cases, school boards. She is the only state library media coordinator and feels overwhelmed by the magnitude of her job. How can she serve the needs of everyone and remain an effective leader? What can she do to encourage each school district to understand the broader issues of school library media services and apply them to their specific needs?

All curriculum and special services coordinators in the state are asked to set goals at the beginning of each school year. The state library media coordinator decides that her primary goal will be to promote the principles of intellectual freedom. Her plan is to offer a series of professional development workshops for library media specialists that deal with the day-to-day issues related to the challenges they face in their schools. The first workshop focuses on *materials selection, developing and using selection policies,* and *the role of the school library media professional in promoting the principles of intellectual freedom in their schools.* Subsequent workshops will deal with *issues of access, labeling, privacy, Internet access,* and *programming issues that challenge the principles of intellectual freedom.* She thinks that the best way to address the very real issues that school library media specialists experience is to ask the workshop participants to send specific scenarios to her. In this way, she is prepared and armed with suggestions for dealing with their special needs.

The state library media coordinator feels that school library media specialists will gain more from professional workshops if they are aware of support documents offered by the American Library Association, such as the Library Bill of Rights. In addition to reading the basic tenets of this document, she also requests that all participants read the following statement from the *Intellectual Freedom Manual* (ALA, 7th edition):

Intellectual freedom can exist only where two essential conditions are met: first, that all individuals have the right to hold any belief on any subject and to convey their ideas in any form they deem appropriate; and second, that society makes an equal commitment to the right of unrestricted access to information and ideas regardless of the communication medium used, the content of the work, and the viewpoints of both the author and receiver of information. Freedom to express oneself through a chosen mode of communication, including the Internet, becomes virtually meaningless if access to that information is not protected. Intellectual freedom implies a circle, and that circle is broken if either freedom of expression or access to ideas is stifled.

CHAPTER 1

Materials Selection

Just as our eyes need light in order to see, our minds need ideas in order to conceive.

Nicolas Malebranche,
French philosopher, 1674

M aterials selection is a core component of the daily responsibilities of a school library media specialist. It is an ongoing job, even in media centers that have excellent collections. Universities teach school library media specialists, administrators, and teachers that the media center is the center of the school—the place where students find materials that support all of their learning needs as well as the place to come for recreational reading and learning. School library media specialists must oversee every aspect of this "center," and they have a professional responsibility to maintain a balanced collection of materials that serves the individual needs of all students and faculty in their schools. This means that materials should represent a wide range of abilities and respect and celebrate the culturally diverse society in which we live. The selection of materials should be objective and completely free of personal bias. To this end, school library media professionals must know that there will be challenges to materials they select, but sound selection guidelines outlined in a materials selection policy provide support for defending such challenges.

The Information Age in which we live has redefined how the school library media center serves the educational and recreational needs of patrons. In the past, fiction and nonfiction print materials, periodicals, newspapers, and reference books have been the core collection of any school library media center. Now, e-books, music CDs, film, computer software, print and nonprint materials in foreign languages, textbooks, college catalogs, and online databases are essential items in the collection of the twenty-first-century school library media center.

Learning Resources

The term *learning resources* refers to any person(s) or any material (whether acquired or locally produced) with instructional content or function that is used for formal or informal teaching/learning purposes. Learning resource materials may include textbooks, other books, charts, maps and globes, models and realia, pictures, games, data files, websites, motion pictures and DVDs, periodicals and monographs, slides, sound recordings, printed music, and transparencies. Community people, agencies, and organizations are vital learning resources, as well as national and international agencies, museums, libraries, and other educational institutions that offer programs via the Internet or satellite.

The primary objective of learning resources is to support, enrich, and help implement the educational program of the school through the interaction of professional personnel and other members of the local and global community. It is the duty of professional staff to provide students with a wide range of materials at varying levels of difficulty, with diversity of appeal, and the presentation of different points of view.

Basic Components of a Selection Policy

**Part 1. Selection of
Library Media Materials**

1. Statement of Policy

2. Objectives for Selection

3. Responsibility of Selection
   a. Delegation of Responsibility to Professional Staff
   b. Particular Responsibilities of Staff Members

4. Selection Criteria
   a. General Selection Criteria
   b. Specific Selection Criteria

5. Policy on Controversial Materials
   a. General Statement
   b. Library Bill of Rights
   c. "The Freedom to Read" statement
   d. ALA "Policy on Confidentiality of Library Records"

**Part 2. Procedures for Selection of
Library Media Materials**

1. Procedures for Implementation
   a. Selection Aids
   b. Outside Recommendation Procedures
   c. Gifts
   d. Special Collections and Concerns

2. Collection Maintenance: Evaluation and Review of Existing Materials

3. Procedures for Dealing with Challenged Materials
   a. Request for Review
   b. The Review Committee
   c. Resolution and Appeal

The Classroom and Library Media Center

A fifth-grade teacher in an elementary school is teaching The Giver *by Lois Lowry to her gifted class. A parent has challenged the book because she does not think the topic of euthanasia is appropriate for her ten-year-old daughter. The principal has asked the library media specialist to handle the challenge. She does not feel comfortable in this role, because she chose not to purchase Lowry's novel for the library collection.*

This is a tough situation; it is difficult for this library media specialist to defend a novel that she did not include in the library's collection. But remember that it is the role of the school library media specialist to uphold the principles of intellectual freedom and to support a teacher's right to teach and select the novels she uses for instruction. Since *The Giver* is considered appropriate for most upper elementary grades, the library media specialist should think about why she did not select the book for the collection. Was she personally offended by the topics and themes of the book? Did she think the book would not appeal to the majority of the students? Was she afraid of potential challenges?

Let's examine two issues:

1. *The role of school library media specialists in dealing with school challenges.* School library media specialists are often called upon to deal with challenges to materials, even those used in the classroom. A school library media professional plays a vital role on a teaching team and should not in any way challenge the teacher's decision to include a specific novel in her curriculum. Pledge support of the teacher and follow this process:

Selection Tools Commonly Used by Schools

ALA Recommended Lists, such as Notable Children's Materials and Best Books for Young Adults

Booklist

Book Links

Bulletin for the Center of Children's Books

Horn Book

Kirkus Reviews

Library Journal

Library Media Connection

Media and Methods

Publisher's Weekly

School Library Journal

Voice of Youth Advocates

H. W. Wilson publications

- Review the school district's selection policy for classroom novel studies. If there is not a policy, ask that one be written so that teachers have support for curriculum materials in the future. See www.ncte.org/action/anti-censorship/rationales/ for Rationales for Teaching Challenged Books and www.ncte.org/positions/statements/selectingelamaterial/ for Guidelines for Selection of Materials in English Language Arts Programs.
- Discuss with the teacher her goals and objectives for teaching the novel in order to understand them fully.
- Help the teacher select an alternative novel for the student to read should the parent request it.
- Arrange a meeting with the teacher, principal, and parent.
- Give the parent a copy of the selection policy and the guidelines for reconsideration of classroom materials.
- Ask the parent to complete a materials reconsideration form.
- Let the parent know the time line for the reconsideration process.
- Make sure that the parent understands that she can request an alternative novel for her child, but that the class will continue studying *The Giver* while the challenge to the book is being considered.

2. *The responsibility of school library media specialists in developing the school library media center collection.* A library media center must serve the entire student body, including their curricular and recreational reading needs. Even if there are only a few students in the school who gravitate to *The Giver,* these students need to know that there are materials in their library media center that interest them and challenge them to think and grow as individuals. In the future, the library media specialist should meet with the faculty and ask them to share the novels they plan to teach. These novels

Specific Criteria for Selection

- Appropriate for recommended age and grade levels in the school
- Supports the curriculum objectives of the instructional program
- Favorable reviews in standard selection sources
- Recommended by faculty
- Accurate and objective
- High artistic quality and/or literary style
- Appropriate for students with varied learning styles
- Represents a variety of viewpoints on controversial subjects

should be purchased for the library media center. For now, the library media specialist should follow these steps as she reconsiders placing Lowry's novel in the library media center's collection:

- Reexamine the reviews of *The Giver*.
- Note the age recommendation.
- Consider the needs of the gifted students in your school.
- Realize that your selection decisions must be objective and free of personal bias.
- Above all, remember that the library media center must serve the entire student body—not just the majority of the students. ■

CASE STUDY 2

Demands of a Specific Curriculum

An English teacher, a social studies teacher, and the art teacher in a high school are planning to team teach a humanities class that connects literature, history, and art. They have asked the library media specialist to purchase art books for the library media center to support their planned curriculum. Currently, the library media center contains very few art books, and the library media specialist recognizes the need for these materials. The principal, who approved the curriculum, is concerned that some of the art books may contain nude images. Though the teachers insist that the books are necessary to support their curriculum objectives, the principal says that he will approve the purchase of the books only if pages with nude images are removed. The library media specialist cannot bring himself to make this promise.

I saw a picture of Michelangelo's statue of David in an encyclopedia in my school library. Someone had used a black magic marker to block out the statue's penis. It made me think that I was looking at something dirty. Then, a family friend who was visiting Italy sent a postcard of David. At this point, I saw art. I hated the person who made me think otherwise—and to think that it happened in my school library.

Age 16

Sample Library Vandalism Statutes

California

§ 19910. Malicious cutting, tearing, defacing, breaking, or injuring.

Any person who maliciously cuts, tears, defaces, breaks, or injures any book, map, chart, picture, engraving, statue, coin, model, apparatus, or other work of literature, art, mechanics, or object of curiosity, deposited in any public library, gallery, museum, collection, fair, or exhibition, is guilty of a misdemeanor.

The parent or guardian of a minor who willfully and maliciously commits any act within the scope of this section shall be liable for all damages so caused by the minor.

Michigan

§ 750.391. Maliciously injuring or mutilating library books.

Maliciously injuring or mutilating library books—Any person who shall wilfully, maliciously or wantonly tear, deface or mutilate or write upon, or by other means injure or mar any book, pamphlet, map, chart, painting, picture, photograph, periodical, newspaper, magazine, manuscript or exhibit or any part thereof belonging to or loaned to any public library, or to the library of any literary, scientific, historical or library society or association, whether incorporated or unincorporated, shall be guilty of a misdemeanor.

South Carolina

§ 16-13-330. Stealing or damaging works of literature or objects of art.

Any person who shall steal or unlawfully take or wilfully or maliciously write upon, cut, tear, deface, disfigure, soil, obliterate, break or destroy, or who shall sell or buy or receive, knowing it to have been stolen, any book, pamphlet, document, newspaper, periodical, map, chart, picture, portrait, engraving, statue, coin, medal, equipment, specimen, recording, film or other work of literature or object of art belonging to or in the care of a library, gallery, museum, collection, exhibition or belonging to or in the care of any department or office of the State or local government, or belonging to or in the care of a library, gallery, museum, collection or exhibition which belongs to any incorporated college or university or which belongs to any institution devoted to educational, scientific, literary, artistic, historical or charitable purposes shall be guilty of a misdemeanor and upon conviction shall be punished by a fine of not more than one hundred dollars or imprisonment for not more than thirty days.

Example of Specific Goals for Materials in Library Media Center

- Meet the individual learning needs, abilities, and learning styles of students.
- Provide background materials to supplement classroom instruction.
- Provide a broad range of materials on controversial issues to help students develop critical analytical skills. These may include topics related to sex and sexuality, drugs and alcohol, weapons, politics, various art genres, and religion.

The most significant element of a school library media center's mission is to serve the curricular demands of the school. Library media specialists must examine every curriculum area and purchase materials to support and extend the course requirements of each specific discipline. A statement in the school district's selection policy regarding this important role should aid in dealing with anxious administrators. It is important to note that the courts have granted school boards and school administrators authority over book selection, but they are not given the power to impose their own personal and political biases.

It is always a good idea to take measures to solve materials selection controversies at the school level. Begin by meeting with the teachers who are proposing the new course. Together, decide how to approach the principal about the issue. Perhaps the principal does not know that a materials selection policy exists. Have this document on hand to let the principal know the criteria and resources used to select new materials for the library media center. Remind the principal that history, art, and literature define the human experience, and that to dismiss or omit any part of it is to deny students the "whole" experience. Most important, ask the principal to think about the following questions:

- What kind of message is sent to students when a school defaces books?
- Will students really respect adults who attempt to re-dress art, history, or literature?
- Can students be expected to understand and value the humanities if they are not allowed to truly experience them?

Point out that it is never appropriate to remove pages from a book. Some states have laws that deal with damaging works of literature, such as marking out words considered by some people to be offensive or removing pages. These laws should be posted in the library so that students, as well as school personnel and parents, are aware of them.

If this issue cannot be solved at the school level, then solicit the help of the school library media coordinator and the language arts and social studies curriculum coordinators at the district level or state level. ■

Applying the Principles of Intellectual Freedom

Connect academic freedom with intellectual freedom. Academic freedom guarantees the teacher's right to teach and to select classroom and library resources for instruction.

Make sure everyone involved understands the right of people in a democratic society to express their concerns and their right to due process in the handling of their complaints.

Explain the obligation of the school district to provide intellectual and physical access to resources that provide for a wide range of abilities and differing points of view.

Define intellectual and physical access when appropriate. Intellectual access includes the right to read, receive, and express ideas and the right to acquire skills to seek out, explore, and examine ideas. Physical access includes being able to locate and retrieve information unimpeded by fees, age limits, separate collections, or other restrictions.

Emphasize the need to place the principles of intellectual and academic freedom above personal opinion, and reason above prejudice, when selecting resources.

Connect intellectual freedom and access. The freedom to express your beliefs or ideas becomes meaningless when others are not allowed to receive or have access to those beliefs or ideas.

Stress the need for teachers and librarians to be free to present students with alternatives if students are to learn and use critical thinking and decision-making skills.

Issues Related to Film

Several high schools offer Holocaust studies as a special topics course. The class is an elective and requires that students read literature and view films set during the Holocaust. The teachers from these high schools share resources and a syllabus. The resources for the class are listed in the syllabus so that students and parents understand the requirements. Schindler's List *is one of the films that the teachers want to use with their students, but none of the high schools own the film. The library media professionals are reluctant to purchase the film because it has an R rating. The teachers insist that the film is needed to support their curriculum.*

This issue is closely related to that in case study 2 and should be handled in a similar way. It is extremely important that a school district's selection policy make the connection between academic freedom and intellectual freedom. In this case, the school board and school administration have granted teachers academic freedom by allowing them to develop this special topics class on the Holocaust and to select the resources to be used. *Schindler's List* is rated R by the Motion Picture Association of America (MPAA), but it is important to note that the rating system of this organization does not consider educational significance when assigning ratings. MPAA and other rating services are private advisory codes and have no legal standing.

It is advisable to include a statement regarding film in the school district's materials selection policy. Although it should be understood that *materials* refers to film, music CDs, and any other media, it is a good idea to have a specific statement regard-

Ratings Systems and the Law

Many people believe that ratings affixed to movies, video games, and music recordings are "law," and that the library media center breaks the law if it collects or provides access to materials rated "mature" or for use by adults only.

This belief is incorrect. The organizations that assign ratings, such as the Motion Picture Association of America (MPAA) and the Entertainment Software Ratings Board (ESRB), are not government agencies, nor are their activities sanctioned by local, state, or federal governments. All are private trade associations whose members produce and distribute movies, games, and music. Each organization administers its ratings program as a benefit for its members, who want to give parents advance information about the movie, game, or song so the parents can decide if the product is appropriate for their child.

An item's rating is meant to serve only as an informative advisory for parents. A rating such as the MPAA's R rating is not, and has never been, a legal determination that a particular motion picture is "obscene," or "obscene as to minors," or "harmful to minors." Only a court of law can make that determination.

Moreover, such ratings systems are strictly voluntary. No law requires filmmakers, game designers, or musicians to submit their work for a rating, and no law requires theaters or retailers to follow the ratings guidelines when selling movie tickets, DVDs, games, or music. Those theater owners and dealers who enforce a ratings system do so voluntarily to provide a service to parents.

Courts have invalidated laws and ordinances that enforce ratings systems as a means of denying minors access to films, games, and other content on the grounds that such restrictions violate minors' First Amendment rights. Among the cases are *Engdahl v. City of Kenosha,* which invalidated a Kenosha, Wisconsin, ordinance that used MPAA ratings to prohibit minors from seeing R-rated films; and *Motion Picture Association of America v. Specter,* which invalidated a Philadelphia criminal ordinance that penalized any theater allowing minors to view films rated "not suitable for children" by the MPAA. More recently, the Seventh Circuit Court of Appeals in Chicago and the Eighth Circuit Court of Appeals in St. Louis invalidated state and local ordinances that used the ESRB's private ratings system to restrict minors' access to video games.

Even though library media specialists may consider an item's rating as one of many factors in the selection process, they should avoid adopting policies that use private content rating systems to restrict students' access to library materials. Instead, they should adopt and promote policies and practices that provide parents with information to guide their children's choices and equip young people themselves with critical viewing and thinking skills that will enable them to make good judgments about the films, music, and games they view and use.

Additional Resources

Access for Children and Young People to Videotapes and Other Nonprint Formats: An Interpretation of the Library Bill of Rights. American Library Association, 1989

American Amusement Mach. Association v. Kendrick, 244 F.3d 954 (7th Cir. 2001)

Engdahl v. City of Kenosha, 317 F. Supp. 1133 (E.D. Wis. 1970)

Free Access for Minors: An Interpretation of the Library Bill of Rights. American Library Association, 1991

Interactive Digital Software Association v. St. Louis County, 329 F.3d 954 (8th Cir. 2003)

Motion Picture Association of America v. Specter, 315 F. Supp. 824 (E.D. Pa. 1970)

Selection of Nonprint Media

Nonprint materials should be evaluated and considered for the library media collection in the same way print materials are selected. These materials are often expensive, and they are not reviewed as widely as print materials. Nonetheless, school library media specialists and classroom teachers should follow these guidelines as they preview nonprint media for the school library media center collection:

- Pertinent to the curriculum
- Age appropriate
- Unbiased, accurate, and current content
- Balanced viewpoints
- Good technical quality

ing the selection of nonprint materials and to have a circulation policy that supports the use of these media. Some school districts do not allow films with R ratings; others restrict the use of such films to classroom use. Many do not allow any students under the age of seventeen to view such a film without parental permission. Requiring parental permission often causes unwarranted attention to what some people view as unsuitable for use in the classroom. Since the Holocaust studies class is an elective, and because the teachers have a course syllabus that specifies the viewing of *Schindler's List,* it is unlikely that parents will lodge a complaint about the use of this film. At least one of the high school media centers should procure the film so that teachers have it readily available to support the curriculum for this special topics class.

Note: Some states require that all high school students take a Holocaust studies course. This does not change the philosophy or methods used to deal with "controversial" films. Course syllabi that include a list of resource requirements may actually serve as a defense should a challenge occur. ■

Selecting Databases

All of the schools in the district are provided a collection of databases funded by the state. Some subscribe to additional databases. Library media specialists fear that some of the content available through these data services is inappropriate for their students. They feel uncomfortable in selecting databases because the scope of the material is so broad and may not be age appropriate.

Databases are a vital part of the school library media center's collection and should be included in the materials selection policy. Like periodicals, newspapers, and other print sources, these databases include information that may not be of interest to all students. Schools subscribe to databases to enhance and support the research needs of students because these services provide access to a greater number of serials and obscure books than most school library media centers can afford. In addition, databases eliminate the need to archive periodicals and newspapers physically and give the media center access to regularly updated information. It is not uncommon for school library media centers to purchase reference books such as biographical dictionaries, encyclopedias, foreign language dictionaries, almanacs, and dictionaries of quotations to augment the reference collection.

Working with teachers and students to help them understand the vast amount of material available to them through data services is pertinent to the success of data usage. Formal and informal workshops help patrons learn to navigate data services and identify content appropriate to their individual needs. Ask students to consider the following questions as they begin a database search:

Tip

Consider the following factors when selecting databases: scope of materials, number of full-text articles, ease in navigation, comprehensive documentation, cost, relevance to curriculum, and availability of off-campus use.

Diversity in Collection Development: An Interpretation of the Library Bill of Rights

Throughout history, the focus of censorship has fluctuated from generation to generation. Books and other materials have not been selected or have been removed from library collections for many reasons, among which are prejudicial language and ideas, political content, economic theory, social philosophies, religious beliefs, sexual forms of expression, and other potentially controversial topics.

Some examples of censorship may include removing or not selecting materials because they are considered by some as racist or sexist; not purchasing conservative religious materials; not selecting materials about or by minorities because it is thought these groups or interests are not represented in a community; or not providing information on or materials from non-mainstream political entities.

Librarians may seek to increase user awareness of materials on various social concerns by many means, including, but not limited to, issuing bibliographies and presenting exhibits and programs. Librarians have a professional responsibility to be inclusive, not exclusive, in collection development and in the provision of interlibrary loan. Access to all materials legally obtainable should be assured to the user, and policies should not unjustly exclude materials even if they are offensive to the librarian or the user. Collection development should reflect the philosophy inherent in Article II of the Library Bill of Rights: "Libraries should provide materials and information presenting all points of view on current and historical issues. Materials should not be proscribed or removed because of partisan or doctrinal disapproval." A balanced collection reflects a diversity of materials, not an equality of numbers. Collection development responsibilities include selecting materials in the languages in common use in the community the library serves. Collection development and the selection of materials should be done according to professional standards and established selection and review procedures.

There are many complex facets to any issue, and variations of context in which issues may be expressed, discussed, or interpreted. Librarians have a professional responsibility to be fair, just, and equitable and to give all library users equal protection in guarding against violation of the library patron's right to read, view, or listen to materials and resources protected by the First Amendment, no matter what the viewpoint of the author, creator, or selector. Librarians have an obligation to protect library collections from removal of materials based on personal bias or prejudice, and to select and support the access to materials on all subjects that meet, as closely as possible, the needs, interests, and abilities of all persons in the community the library serves. This includes materials that reflect political, economic, religious, social, minority, and sexual issues.

Intellectual freedom, the essence of equitable library services, provides for free access to all expressions of ideas through which any and all sides of a question, cause, or movement may be explored. Toleration is meaningless without tolerance for what some may consider detestable. Librarians cannot justly permit their own preferences to limit their degree of tolerance in collection development, because freedom is indivisible.

Adopted July 14, 1982; amended January 10, 1990 by the ALA Council

- Why do I need the information?
- What type of information do I need?
- Do I need conflicting viewpoints?
- Am I looking for historical data or more current information?
- Do I need primary resources? ∎

CASE STUDY 5

Individual Needs of Students

English-language learning (ELL) is the primary focus of the reading instructional program in an elementary school that serves a large Latino community. Most of the students do well with English, but their parents cannot help them practice reading because of their own English deficiencies. The PTA is pressuring the school to purchase library books in Spanish. The principal insists that the library budget is too small to purchase these materials and suggests that the parents get a public library card and use the resources there. Many of the parents do not have transportation and cannot make use of the public library services. The library media specialist feels caught between the principal and the PTA.

Schools promote parental involvement in their children's education and should never impede a parent's ability to take part. Most school library media budgets are small and cannot meet all of the resource demands of the school and its community in one budget year. But the library media specialist and the principal should make a plan to

Helpful Websites

Center for the Study of Books in Spanish for Children and Adolescents: www.csusm.edu/campus_centers/csb/

National Association for Bilingual Education: www.nabe.org

REFORMA: www.reforma.org

Teachers of English to Speakers of Other Languages (TESOL): www.tesol.org

accommodate the needs of these students and their families. It is in the best interest of students and their parents to know about the services of the public library, but the mission of a school library is to support the resource needs of the school community. Therefore, since the school serves a heavily Latino population, it is necessary to purchase Spanish-language materials for the library media center collection.

There are several ways a library media center can serve its Latino and Spanish-speaking population in school, such as these:

- Purchase a specified number of Spanish-language books each year. In a few years, the library media center will have an acceptable collection.
- Search for books and materials that celebrate the cultural heritage of the Latino students in the schools (e.g., Pura Belpré Award).
- Meet with appropriate staff at the public library and ask if the school might borrow a small collection of books in Spanish for use with non-English-speaking parents.
- Search for grants to fund the purchase of materials in Spanish.
- Elicit guidance for resources and programming ideas from such organizations as REFORMA (National Association to Promote Library Services to Latinos and the Spanish Speaking).
- Develop a program within the school community where older students who have mastered English might tutor students and their parents in reading.
- Allow students to become teachers by asking them to make a picture dictionary in English and Spanish that they might share with their families. ∎

Extracurricular Needs of Students

A high school debate team is scheduled to argue several controversial subjects: same-sex marriage, abortion, gun control, school prayer, and sex education in schools. Several students have expressed concern that there are not enough materials in the media center to support their arguments. The debate team sponsor proposed the topics, but he told the students that materials on these topics might be too controversial for the school's media center collection. The students feel that they should not have to go to another library to find the materials they need.

The debate team sponsor should be informed that the mission of the school library media center is to support the educational needs of the students, regardless of the controversial nature of their needs. Do not confuse "educational needs" with curriculum. The debate team is school-sponsored; therefore, its members should expect the same level of access to materials and information as students engaged in core curriculum areas. A statement regarding library media services to school clubs and special groups like debate teams, forensic groups, and school newspaper staffs should be specifically defined in the school's faculty and student handbook. In this way, students and faculty know what type of services they can expect from the library media center.

More specific ways to support the debate team:

- Ask the debate team coach to provide a list of topics that the students need to research.
- Do a bibliographic search of available materials in the school's library media center, including print, nonprint, reference sources, and databases.

Board of Education v. Pico—The School Library and the First Amendment

In 1976, members of the Island Trees School Board directed school officials to remove ten books from the school district's high school and junior high school libraries. The board members characterized the removed books as "anti-American, anti-Christian, anti-Semitic, and just plain filthy" and asserted that the books' removal was necessary to protect the district's students. Among the books ordered removed were Kurt Vonnegut's *Slaughter-house-Five,* Langston Hughes's *Best Short Stories of Negro Writers,* the nominally anonymous *Go Ask Alice,* Alice Childress's *A Hero Ain't Nothin' but a Sandwich,* and Eldridge Cleaver's *Soul on Ice.*

A group of students led by Steven Pico filed a lawsuit to challenge the school board's actions, asserting that the board's decision to remove the books violated students' First Amendment rights. The board argued that both law and tradition had vested it with broad authority to control the curriculum, including the materials available in the school library. The lawsuit eventually reached the U.S. Supreme Court.

In 1982, the Supreme Court decided *Board of Education, Island Trees Union Free School District No. 26. v. Pico.* The decision stands today as the principal legal authority concerning censorship in the public school library.

The Court acknowledged that local school boards enjoy broad discretion to manage school affairs and to make decisions concerning school curriculum. It cautioned, however, that the school board is required to exercise its discretion within the limits imposed by the First Amendment and the Constitution.

The Court further held that "First Amendment rights, applied in light of the special characteristics of the school environment, are available to students" and explicitly recognized the student's right to receive information in the library media center. The Court stated that "the right to receive ideas is a necessary predicate to the recipient's meaningful exercise of his own right of speech, press and political freedom" and identified the school library as the principal locus of the student's freedom "to inquire, to study and to evaluate."

The Court distinguished between the school board's broad discretion to prescribe classroom curriculum and the "unique role of the school library":

> Petitioners emphasize the inculcative function of secondary education, and argue that they must be allowed unfettered discretion to "transmit community values" through the Island Trees schools. But that sweeping claim overlooks the unique role of the school library. It appears from the record that use of the Island Trees school libraries is completely voluntary on the part of students. Their selection of books from these libraries is entirely a matter of free choice; the libraries afford them an opportunity at self-education and individual enrichment that is wholly optional. Petitioners might well defend their claim of absolute discretion in matters of curriculum by reliance upon their duty to inculcate community values. But we think that petitioners' reliance upon that duty is misplaced where, as here, they attempt to extend their claim of absolute discretion beyond the compulsory environment of the classroom, into the school library and the regime of voluntary inquiry that there holds sway.

The Court then described the limits placed upon the school board's authority to remove books from the school library:

> Petitioners rightly possess significant discretion to determine the content of their school libraries. But that discretion may not be exercised in a narrowly partisan or political manner. . . . Our Constitution does not permit the official suppression of ideas. Thus whether petitioners' removal of books from their school libraries denied respondents their First Amendment rights depends upon the motivation behind petitioners' actions. *If petitioners intended by their removal decision to deny respondents access to ideas with which petitioners disagreed, and if this intent was the decisive factor in petitioners' decision, then petitioners have exercised their discretion in violation of the Constitution.* (emphasis added)

Having established the standard for evaluating the student plaintiffs' claims, the Court examined the evidence and found that there was a genuine issue as to whether the school board had violated the First Amendment rights of the students. The Court pointed to board members' statements that the removed books were "anti-American" and "offensive to . . . Americans in general" as proof of the board's improper motivation.

The Court said that further proof of the board's bad intent could be found in its failure to use an established and unbiased procedure to review the challenged books. According to the record established in the case, the school board ignored its own established policy for reviewing controversial materials and disregarded the advice and information provided by the superintendent of schools, the librarians and teachers within the Island Trees school district, literary experts, and professional publications.

The Court carefully noted that its decision was not intended to alter or limit the school board's discretion in adding books to the library and said it would be permissible to remove books if the sole basis for removal was concern about a book's "educational suitability" or whether the book was "pervasively vulgar." But if the decisive factor in removing a book was the board's disagreement with the ideas contained in the book, or a desire to impose orthodoxy in matters of politics, religion, or other matters of opinion, such a decision would be unconstitutional.

The Court's opinion in *Pico* remains vital today. Books and other materials acquired by the public school library through its established selection process are protected speech, and the student's right to read and consult those materials is protected by the First Amendment. If a school board undertakes to remove a book or other library materials from the school library, it must do so on the basis of established and unbiased policies and procedures.

Courts uniformly apply the reasoning used in *Pico* to resolve censorship controversies in libraries, carefully examining to see if a decision to remove a book or other materials is motivated by a desire to suppress or eliminate disfavored ideas and viewpoints. In so doing, the courts seek to preserve each student's "freedom to inquire, to study and to evaluate, to gain new maturity and understanding."

Additional Resources

Board of Education, Island Trees Union Free School District No. 26, v. Pico, 457 U.S. 853 (1982)

Case v. Unified School District No. 233, 908 F. Supp. 864 (D. Kan. 1995)

Counts v. Cedarville School District, 295 F. Supp. 2d 996 (W.D. Ark. 2003)

- Consider interlibrary loan to fill voids in the collection.
- Plan a special session with the debate team to point out materials available in their library.
- Plan a workshop with students and faculty to teach them how to navigate the databases available in the library media center. Include skills in identifying reliable Internet sites.
- Make a note of the voids in the collection and search for materials to fill these voids as the budget allows. ∎

Needs of All Students

A middle school student asked help in locating a novel about the gay/lesbian lifestyle. A search of the library media center's catalog revealed a void in the collection. There was only one novel for this student. The library media specialist admits that she may have been remiss in selecting gay/lesbian novels but wonders what the principal and community would say if they thought the library was promoting these materials.

The purpose of a school library media center is to serve students, not to condone or condemn any of their information or reading requests. Perhaps the student is questioning her sexuality and needs a novel to give her the courage to let her friends and family know. Maybe she is seeking knowledge about a lifestyle that is unknown to her. She may have a friend or family member who is gay, and she wants to understand them better. It does not matter why the student wants the material, and it is not the role of the library media specialist to ask. It is the role of the library media professional to honor the request of the student and to take measures to fill the void in the collection. Selection is an inclusive process in which school library media specialists seek materials with a broad range of viewpoints and subject matter. Because an item is selected does not mean the school library media specialist endorses or promotes it. She is simply helping the library fulfill its mission of providing information with all points of view.

The same criteria should be used in selecting these materials as in selecting all other materials. *Booklist, School Library Journal,* and *VOYA* have at times featured gay/lesbian materials for children and young adults. Refer to back issues of these review sources to begin building a solid collection of gay/lesbian materials. Then, add new materials as they become available. In the meantime, help the student locate materials at the public library or offer to find novels through interlibrary loan.

A library media professional should refer to the mission of the school and to the school district's materials selection policy to answer the question about dealing with the community and the school administrator. Most schools and school districts state in their mission that they "serve the *needs* of all students." "All" means all genders, all ethnic groups, all students who are gay, straight, or handicapped. There should be no discrimination or bias expressed in the library collection or in the services provided by the library media center. ∎

In talking with middle school students during Banned Books Week, I pointed out examples of books that have been challenged. One of the books was *Annie on My Mind* by Nancy Garden. After class, an eighth-grade girl followed me to the library and asked for Garden's book. I helped her locate it, and she checked it out. Two days later she appeared back in the library and said, "I read this book, and I'm glad I did. I've always had a prejudice against the gay/lesbian lifestyle. Now I see it differently."

Court Opinion

Stevana Case, et al., Plaintiffs, vs. Unified School District No. 233, Johnson County, Kansas, et al., Defendants.

United States District Court for the District of Kansas
908 F. Supp. 864 (1995)
Opinion by: Judge G. T. Van Bebber [Edited for length]

Introduction

This case involves plaintiffs' challenge of the decision of the Board of Education of Unified School District No. 233 of Johnson County, Kansas, and its superintendent to remove a book entitled *Annie on My Mind* from the school libraries. Plaintiffs' claims, brought pursuant to 42 U.S.C. § 1983, allege that defendants violated plaintiffs' rights under the First and Fourteenth Amendments to the United States Constitution and § 11 of the Bill of Rights to the Kansas Constitution. Plaintiffs seek injunctive and declaratory relief.

A trial to the court was held on September 20, 21, 22, and October 4, 1995. After careful consideration of the evidence and arguments in this case, the court concludes that defendants unconstitutionally removed *Annie on My Mind* from the school libraries.

Pursuant to Fed. R. Civ. P. 52(a), the court makes the following findings of fact and conclusions of law.

The Removal of *Annie on My Mind*

During 1993, the Gay and Lesbian Alliance Against Defamation/Kansas City (GLAAD/KC) and Project 21 engaged in the promotion of so-called gay and lesbian issues in the Kansas City metropolitan area.

On March 15, 1993, Project 21 circulated questionnaires to Olathe School Board member candidates asking for their views on certain gay and lesbian issues. Project 21 also advised the candidates of its purposes and agenda.

In the summer of 1993, GLAAD/KC and Project 21 notified the Olathe School District's media specialists[1] that they were launching a book project to insure that students had access to diverse information regarding gender and sexual orientation.

On or about July 16, 1993, the Regional Coordinator of Project 21, Robert Birle, wrote Dr. Wimmer and requested the identity of the district representative to whom he could send curriculum materials and resource information concerning sexual orientation (including heterosexuality, bisexuality and homosexuality).

On or about August 9, 1993, Robert Birle, on behalf of GLAAD/KC and Project 21, wrote Dr. Wimmer and offered to donate two books with gay or lesbian story lines to the District. The books were *Annie on My Mind* by Nancy Garden and *All American Boys* by Frank Mosca.

Annie on My Mind is a novel depicting a fictional romantic relationship between two teenage girls. *Annie* has received numerous literary awards and distinctions, including an American Library Association award for

"Best of the Best" books for young adults. The book contains no vulgarity, offensive language, or explicit sexual content.

In October 1993, Birle delivered copies of *Annie on My Mind* and *All American Boys* to each of the three Olathe School District high schools.

The Project 21 book donation to the Olathe School District and other local school districts received extensive media coverage in the Kansas City metropolitan area, and school district representatives received a number of telephone calls from the public, presumably prompted by the media coverage.

On October 6, 1993, Loretta Wood, the Olathe East High School media specialist, notified Dr. Alison Banikowski, the District's Assistant Superintendent for Curriculum and Instruction, that the District's online library catalog indicated that prior to the donation, the Olathe South High School library had two copies of *Annie on My Mind* on its shelves. School officials later discovered that copies of *Annie* also were located in the collections at Olathe East High School, Pioneer Trail Junior High School, and Indian Trail Junior High School, and had been on the library shelves of those schools prior to the book donations. Copies of *Annie* were not located in any other Olathe School District library. No copies of *All American Boys* were located in any of the District's libraries.

Trial testimony indicated that copies of *Annie* were on the District's library shelves for a number of years. Some of the copies had been on the shelves since the mid-1980s. The evidence does not show that anyone checked out or read the District's copies of *Annie* prior to the dispute involved in this case.

On October 8, 1993, Dr. Banikowski requested Loretta Wood and the other media specialists of the District to review the donated books and to advise her of their conclusions as to the suitability of the book for inclusion in the District's library collections.

The librarians examined and compiled national book reviews of *Annie on My Mind*. These generally were found to be favorable reviews of the book.

On or about October 25, 1993, Jeffrey Blair, a media specialist at Olathe South High School, sent a memorandum to Loretta Wood advising that he had reviewed both of the donated books. Blair found *Annie on My Mind* to be of value, but not *All American Boys*. He described the characters in *Annie* as "fully rounded and believable." Blair was concerned about the lack of reference to communicable diseases and AIDS in either book. He pointed out that *Annie* was currently on the shelves at Olathe South. Blair recommended that the school keep *Annie* on the shelf, but that the school should not add *All American Boys* to the collection. The latter book had not been a part of the district's collection.

Loretta Wood then wrote a memorandum to Dr. Banikowski in which she gave *Annie on My Mind* a favorable review. Wood found the book "sensitive and realistic." In contrast, Wood described *All American Boys* as "shallow and incomplete."

Media coverage continued regarding the Project 21 book donations. The *Kansas City Star* reported that protesters burned copies of *Annie on My Mind* on the steps of the Kansas City School District offices. The article also reported that copies of *Annie on My Mind* had been on the shelves of the Olathe South High School since the mid-1980s.

On or about October 26, 1993, Dr. Banikowski reported to Dr. Wimmer that the continuing media coverage had prompted her to organize a meeting on November 1, 1993, with all media specialists to discuss and review the donated books.

On November 1, 1993, Dr. Banikowski and Dr. Patricia All, the Executive Director of Education and Technology for the Olathe School District, met with the District's secondary media specialists (high school librarians) to discuss the results of their review of the donated books. All media specialists agreed that *Annie on My Mind* was an appropriate book for the high school library collections, but that *All American Boys* was not appropriate. The media specialists were in agreement that *Annie* had literary merit and that other reviews were quite favorable.

Dr. Banikowski advised Dr. Wimmer of the outcome of the media specialists' review. She indicated that she would return the copies of *All American Boys.*

On November 9, 1993, Dr. Banikowski wrote Robert Birle and advised him that the District had accepted the donation of *Annie on My Mind,* but had not accepted *All American Boys.*

On November 11, 1993, Dr. Wimmer informed Board of Education members Janet Simpson and Ron Hinkle that the District had received copies of the two books from Project 21, that the District had initiated its book review procedures, and that the library review committee had recommended acceptance of *Annie on My Mind* and rejection of *All American Boys.* Dr. Wimmer also stated that he had not received any formal complaints from parents regarding the books. Dr. Wimmer provided a copy of *Annie on My Mind* to Board members Simpson and Hinkle so that they could read the book.

Dr. Wimmer met with Dr. Banikowski and Dr. All and determined that the District needed to clarify procedures on donated books. Dr. Wimmer also wanted to discuss the public concern regarding the donated books.

On December 10, 1993, Dr. Wimmer indicated in a memorandum called "board notes" sent to Board of Education members that he had scheduled a meeting with the media specialists in order to make a "final disposition" of the book donation issue.

During the weekend prior to the meeting with the District's media specialists, Dr. Wimmer prepared a set of "Book Donation Guidelines." Dr. Wimmer did not seek input from anyone in the preparation of these guidelines.

Dr. Wimmer and Dr. Banikowski met with the secondary media specialists on December 13, 1993, and at the meeting Dr. Wimmer disseminated his new book donation guidelines. Dr. Wimmer had decided prior to this meeting that the District would not only refuse the books donated by Project 21, but that existing copies of *Annie on My Mind* would be removed from the District's libraries. Dr. Wimmer did not have any meetings or consultations with the District's media specialists prior to making his decision to remove *Annie on My Mind* from the District's libraries.

Following his explication of the new book donation guidelines, Dr. Wimmer informed the media specialists that *Annie on My Mind* was to be removed from the District libraries. Dr. Banikowski asked the media specialists to send all copies of *Annie* to her office.

Although the District had not received written complaints from anyone about *Annie on My Mind*, Dr. Wimmer told the media specialists that the District needed to take action because of community concerns regarding the issue. Dr. Banikowski and the District office had received numerous phone calls protesting the fact that *Annie on My Mind* was on the library shelves.

Dr. Wimmer also advised the media specialists that he did not believe that the Board of Education would support acceptance of the book donation. Based upon his experience in working with the Board members, Dr. Wimmer felt that a majority of the Board "would favor taking this book off the shelves."

Dr. Wimmer testified that "the book in and of itself was not—nor the content of the book was not a high criteria in regard to my decision. It was all of the issues that were related and surrounding to that." Dr. Wimmer further explained that those issues were:

> Project 21 and the turmoil that primarily . . . was created in the media and the constant distraction that we were encoun-

tering in terms of trying to focus on what we really were all about at the time. I was trying to make a determination that would try to put that into some frame of reference, and deemphasize the focus that was being placed on that issue.

Dr. Wimmer removed the book from District libraries in part because he believed Project 21 was using the book to promote the group's agenda—introduction of information about homosexuality into the curriculum—which was creating controversy. Dr. Wimmer concluded that removing the book would keep the District from being "embroiled into this situation" and would not be adverse to the interests of students because, in his perception, the book did not appear to have been used.

There was no discussion in Dr. Wimmer's meeting with the media specialists about the literary merit or educational suitability of *Annie on My Mind*. Neither did they discuss whether the subject matter of *Annie on My Mind* was appropriate for high school or junior high students. Dr. Wimmer and the media specialists did not discuss alternatives to removal of the book, such as placement on a restricted shelf.

Following the meeting with Dr. Wimmer, the Olathe School District media specialists removed all existing copies of *Annie on My Mind* from the District's library shelves.

On December 16, 1993, Dr. Wimmer distributed the new book donation guidelines to the District's principals and media specialists. Dr. Wimmer felt the guidelines would assist administrators in handling difficult situations.

On or about January 4, 1994, plaintiff Amanda Greb and other District students asked permission to speak at the January 6, 1994, school board meeting to express their views regarding the removal of *Annie on My Mind* from the District's libraries. The students' names were placed on the Board agenda. The Board met in regular session on January 6, 1994. During the meeting, several individuals, including plaintiffs Amanda Greb, Stevana Case, and Sam Pierron, addressed the Board on whether *Annie on My Mind* should be removed from the District libraries. Presentations were made both for and against removal of the book. Everyone who indicated a desire to speak on the issue was permitted to address the Board.

Prior to the January 6, 1994 Board of Education meeting, Dr. Wimmer advised the Board that they should not respond publicly to comments made at the meeting. Dr. Wimmer also recommended that if the Board wished to take a position on the book removal issue, the Board should adjourn to executive session prior to a vote to consult with their attorney. Following the presentations, the Board

adjourned to an executive session to consult with counsel and remained in executive session for thirty minutes. During the executive session, the Board heard presentations from Dr. Wimmer and the Board's counsel regarding the issues surrounding the removal decision. At no time did the Board discuss the literary merit or educational suitability of *Annie on My Mind*.

Prior to the board meeting, Dr. Wimmer had provided the Board with a packet of materials that included a December 30, 1993, letter from the Olathe School District's counsel. The letter advised the Board about First Amendment issues associated with the removal of a book from school libraries. In the letter, the District's counsel advised the Board that a local school board must exercise its discretion "in a manner that complies with the First Amendment." Counsel also stated that "the special characteristics of the school library make that environment especially appropriate for the recognition of the First Amendment rights of Students." Counsel suggested that "if the decisive factor for the removal decision was the 'educational suitability' of the book in question, then its removal would be permissible." The term "education suitability" had not appeared in any of defendants' documents or discussions prior to counsel's letter.

After the Board returned to open session from its executive session, Board member

Hinkle moved to support Dr. Wimmer's decision to remove *Annie on My Mind* from the district's school libraries. Board member Marriott seconded the motion. Without further discussion the Board voted four to two in favor of the motion. Board members Dr. Robert Drummond, Ronald Hinkle, Richard Marriott, and Janet Simpson voted to remove the book. Board members Kevin Hammeke and Steven Hougland opposed the removal. Board member Frank Taylor was not present at the meeting and did not vote on the book removal. As previously noted, the Board members did not engage in any public discussion of their views regarding the book removal and did not address any of the comments the public had made prior to the Board's vote on the issue.

On January 11, 1994, Dr. Wimmer met with students, including plaintiffs Amanda Greb and Sam Pierron, at Olathe South High School to discuss the decision to remove *Annie* from school libraries in the District. Dr. Wimmer told the students that the book had been removed not because a special interest group had donated it, but because leaving the book on the shelf would keep the School District embroiled in controversy.

Motivation for the Removal

Board Member Richard Marriott testified that he voted to remove *Annie on My Mind* because he felt the content of the book was very shallow and very offensive. He was offended by the book's "glorification of the gay lifestyle." He believed that in order for the book not to glorify that lifestyle, "the entire theme would have to be changed." Marriott agreed with the following comments made in a letter written to him:

> There is absolutely no confirmation in the scientific world that homosexuality is a normal or genetic way of life. Therefore, there is absolutely no reason to pass the information to our teens in support of these claims. I do not believe that homosexuality is a normal way of life; I believe it is a choice. Unfortunately, I also believe that it is a choice that destroys healthy sexuality, self image, and obviously leads to a [*sic*] onslaught of physical destruction.

Marriott testified that if the Board allowed the book to remain on the shelf, the community would have looked upon that as the Board of Education's endorsement or approval of a homosexual lifestyle.

Board member Robert Drummond testified that he voted to remove *Annie on My Mind* because he felt that the book was inappropriate and unsuitable for students because it "glorifies and promotes" homosexuality. Drummond testified, "I think part of the theme running through the book, as I recall, is continual tacit endorsement of that particular lifestyle, that it's okay, that it's something that is very acceptable and very typical, very, again, okay." Drummond believed that *Annie on My Mind* "promotes homosexuality." He testified that homosexuality is a mental disorder, immoral, and contrary to the teachings of the Bible and the Christian church. He further stated that homosexuality is a mental disorder similar to schizophrenia or depression. Drummond voted to remove *Annie on My Mind* because he believed the book glorified a lifestyle that is sinful in the eyes of God.

Board member Ronald Hinkle testified that he voted to remove *Annie on My Mind* because he did not think the book was educationally significant or suitable for students. Hinkle testified that he believed that the book had little or no value and that it was not particularly well written. In Hinkle's view, the "book did not seem to give a realistic treatment of the subject matter, and that relates back to promotion and glorification." Hinkle felt the book was not realistic "because it didn't deal with some of the practicalities that homosexuals have to deal with and face. Again, in reference to potential disease, potential death [*sic*]. It just didn't even address those issues, let alone broken relationships with family, friends, et cetera."

When asked why he thought the book was not well written, Hinkle responded: "I'm not defining 'well written' in the sense that the English language is abused at all. There's proper sentence structure and all of that, so in that sense, I'm not saying the book is not well-written. I'm saying the particular theme and the purpose of the book was, I thought, very shallow. I thought it was very shallow." Hinkle believed that the book was shallow because: "There's not a whole lot of in-depth thought or consideration about the particular subject matter. It seemed to have one goal . . . to say that it's okay to be gay, don't worry about it. That seemed to be thrust. And in that sense, I didn't think the book was well written."

Hinkle testified that it is not "okay" to be gay, "because engaging in a gay lifestyle can lead to death, destruction, disease, emotional problems." Hinkle concluded that one of the basic reasons he did not think the book was educationally suitable was because it promoted or glorified the homosexual lifestyle, which "does not meet the basic moral standards of the community." Hinkle believes that in his community, one must be heterosexual in order to meet community moral standards. Hinkle also voted to remove the book because he believed that if the book had been left on the shelf, the public would perceive that as the school board's endorsement or advocation of a homosexual lifestyle.

Board member Janet Simpson testified that she voted to remove *Annie on My Mind* from the District's libraries because she believed that schools should stay completely away from the subject of homosexuality. Simpson concluded that the book was well written, but was objectionable because "it was promoting a very unhealthy lifestyle."

Simpson found the book educationally unsuitable because "it glorified homosexuality as a lifestyle." Simpson stated that she believes homosexuality is unnatural. Simpson testified that the only books about homosexuality she would find educationally suitable are those that would instruct that homosexuality is unhealthy and that would contain "statistics and actual case studies of the results of homosexuality on the mental, physical, emotional, and social well-being of adolescents from entering adolescence to adulthood."

She stated that she believes the library should contain only factual books,[2] which would not include *Annie* or other works of fiction, but would include the Bible because she believes that everything in the Bible is factual.

Simpson believed she had a mandate from patrons in the District to remove the book because it conflicted with the District's values, which are "traditional family values." Simpson testified that she believes in the Bible, and what the Bible says about homosexuality and creationism in the book of Genesis.

Board member Steve Hougland testified that he voted against the removal of *Annie on My Mind* on freedom of speech grounds.

Board member Kevin Hammeke testified that he voted against removal of *Annie* from the District libraries because he believed it was a First Amendment issue.

The District's Policies and Procedures

The Olathe School District libraries use a computer catalog system. The school libraries allow books to be loaned to other libraries within the district.

Only students and faculty may check out materials from the school libraries. A student must be enrolled in a school to check out books from that school's library. Students in the District may check out books from other libraries in the District through an interlibrary loan system.

The Olathe School District hosts a "Media Center Night" no more frequently than one night per week. At Media Center Night, students and their parents may use the high school libraries on a limited basis.

The primary purpose of Media Center Night is to allow current students to perform research, write papers, and meet with teachers.

The Olathe School District has adopted a written "Media Selection Policy," which is included in the District's procedures manual. Dr. Wimmer and his staff developed and adopted the media selection policy pursuant to the Board's delegation of authority to Dr. Wimmer to create and adopt administrative procedures. The media selection policy sets forth the District's selection criteria for library resources. The policy incorporates the American Library Association's School Library Bill of Rights, which states that it is the responsibility of the school library media center to provide materials that: support the curriculum; encourage students' "growth in knowledge" and "development of literary, cultural and aesthetic appreciation and ethical standards"; and "reflect the ideas and beliefs of religious, social, political, historical, and ethnic groups and their contribution to the American and world heritage and culture, thereby enabling students to develop an intellectual integrity in forming judgment." Dr. Wimmer agrees with the policy and believes it should be followed. Historically, the District has followed this policy in addressing complaints or concerns regarding library materials.

The media selection policy also contains procedures for the reconsideration of challenged media. This policy is now and was in effect at all relevant times. The media selection policy sets out a 13-step written procedure to address concerns about library materials. The process begins when a patron challenges the appropriateness of the materials and notifies a teacher, media specialist, or principal. If the building principal is unable to resolve the complaint informally without the removal of the item, the complaint is referred to the appropriate library media coordinator, who appoints a committee to review the complaint. The committee is charged with reading the challenged material and evaluating it according to the District's established criteria for the selection of library materials. The committee issues a report, which is furnished to the building principal, who is responsible for implementing the committee's decision. The complainant is notified of the District's disposition of the complaint. If dissatisfied, the complainant may appeal to the superintendent.

The District failed to follow its adopted procedures for the reconsideration of library materials. The District neither awaited a formal complaint, nor appointed a committee to consider the removal (as opposed to the donation) of *Annie on My Mind.* If the media specialists' committee that was established to consider the donations also acted as a review committee for materials already on the shelves, its recommendation was ignored. The District's written guidelines forbid a reversal of the Review Committee's decision without an appeal to the superintendent by a complainant. No appeal was made. The District also ignored its own incorporation of the American Library Association's Library Bill of Rights, which affirms the importance of having a diversity of ideas available in the library "thereby enabling students to develop an intellectual integrity in forming judgment."

After the media specialists had concluded that the donation of *Annie on My Mind* should be accepted and that the books should be added to the existing copies on the shelves, Dr. Wimmer overrode that decision by promulgating new "book donation guidelines." Dr. Wimmer used the new book donation guidelines to rationalize the refusal of the donation and to remove existing copies of *Annie on My Mind* from the shelves, even though his newly devised donation policy did not cover the removal action. In doing so, he disregarded the recommendation of the media specialists as well as the District's established criteria for the reevaluation of library resources.

In voting to affirm Dr. Wimmer's decision and remove *Annie on My Mind,* the Board of Education did not follow the reconsideration policy, which requires that challenged materials be evaluated according to the District's established criteria for the selection of library materials. There was no discussion by the Board concerning the literary or educational merit of the book. The Board of Education ignored its own guidelines and criteria established for the reconsideration of library materials.

Conclusions of Law

The remaining plaintiffs are current Olathe School District students Andy Case and Jon Stonger and their parents Steven Case and Rex Stonger. Plaintiff Steven Case also claims standing in his capacity as an Olathe School District teacher. After carefully evaluating the standing of the remaining plaintiffs, the court concludes that these current students and their parents have standing to challenge the removal of *Annie on My Mind.*

Andy Case and Jon Stonger had access to *Annie* at the time of its removal from their respective high school or junior high libraries either because the book actually was present on the shelves or because it was available through interlibrary loan. Injunctive and declaratory relief would redress the injury because their access to the book from the school library would be restored.

In addition, Steven Case, in his capacity as a teacher, has standing to challenge the book removal. Steven Case had access to the school library before the removal of *Annie on My Mind* for his personal and professional use. He had the ability to check out books and to assign readings to his students. The court concludes that Steven Case has standing as a teacher to challenge the book's removal. See *Salvail v. Nashua Bd. of Educ.,* 469 F. Supp. 1269 (D.N.H. 1979) (faculty subclass was proper plaintiff); *Right to Read Defense Comm. v. School Comm.,* 454 F. Supp. 703 (D. Mass. 1978) (plaintiffs included librarian and teacher).

Having resolved the standing issues, the court now must address the claims of plaintiffs that defendants' removal of *Annie on My Mind* from the District's libraries violated plaintiffs' rights under the First and Fourteenth Amendments.

First Amendment Claim

Although local school boards have broad discretion in the management of school affairs, they must act within fundamental constitutional limits. See *Board of Educ. v. Pico,* 457 U.S. 853, 863–65, 73 L. Ed. 2d 435, 102 S. Ct. 2799 (1982) (citing *Meyer v. Nebraska,* 262 U.S. 390, 402, 67 L. Ed. 1042, 43 S. Ct. 625 [1923] and *Tinker v. Des Moines Independent Community Sch. Dist.,* 393 U.S. 503, 507, 21 L. Ed. 2d 731, 89 S. Ct. 733 [1969]). In *Pico,* the United States Supreme Court addressed the very issue that confronts the court in the present case: Does the First Amendment impose any limitations upon the discretion of school officials to remove library books from high school and junior high libraries? In a plurality opinion, the Court concluded there are limits. *Id.* at 871–72.

The *Pico* plaintiffs challenged the school board's removal of nine books from the school's libraries. A majority of the Court agreed that genuine issues of material fact precluded summary judgment in favor of the school board. *Id.* at 875–76, 883. Writing for the plurality, Justice Brennan opined that the motivations of school officials would be unconstitutional if the school officials "intended by their removal decision to deny respondents access to ideas with which [the officials] disagreed, and if this intent was the decisive factor in [the removal] decision." *Id.* at 871. The plurality went on to hold that "local school boards may not remove books from school library shelves simply because they dislike the ideas contained in those books and seek by their removal to 'prescribe what shall be orthodox in politics, nationalism, religion, or other matters of opinion.'" *Id.* at 872 (quoting *West Virginia State Bd. of Educ. v. Barnette,* 319 U.S. 624, 642, 87 L. Ed. 1628, 63 S. Ct. 1178 [1943]). The *Pico* plurality indicated that removal may be permissible if the book contained "pervasive vulgarity" or if the book was "educationally unsuitable." *Id.*

Writing separately, Justice Blackmun disagreed with the plurality's assertion that school children have a "right to receive information." *Id.* at 875–79 (concurring opinion).

Instead, he focused on the school board's denial of access to ideas. Justice Blackmun would hold that "school officials may not remove books for the purpose of restricting access to the political ideas or social perspectives discussed in them, when the action is motivated simply by the officials' disapproval of the ideas involved." *Id.* at 879–80 (concurring opinion).

The plurality decision in *Pico* is not binding precedent. *United States v. Friedman,* 528 F.2d 784 (10th Cir. 1976), judgment vacated on other grounds, 430 U.S. 925 (1977); *Campbell v. St. Tammany Parish Sch. Bd.,* 64 F.3d 184, 189 (5th Cir. 1995). The court notes, however, that this is the only Supreme Court decision dealing specifically with the removal of books from a public school library. The court also notes that there are no Tenth Circuit Court of Appeals decisions directly on point. Thus, the court concludes that it should follow the *Pico* decision in analyzing the Olathe School District's removal of *Annie on My Mind* from the District's libraries. *Case v. Unified Sch. Dist. No. 233,* 895 F. Supp. 1463, 1469 (D. Kan. 1995); see *Campbell,* 64 F.3d at 189.

In a recent Fifth Circuit decision, the court reversed the district court's grant of summary judgment in favor of plaintiffs who challenged the school board's removal of a book from the school library. *Campbell,* 64 F.3d at 191. The Fifth Circuit agreed that *Pico* should guide its book removal analysis. The court of appeals remanded the case for trial and directed the district court to determine the "actual motivation" behind the school board's removal of the book, *Voodoo & Hoodoo. Id.* The court made the following observation in the path to its decision to remand:

> In light of the special role of the school library as a place where students may freely and voluntarily explore diverse topics, the School Board's noncurricular decision to remove a book well after it had been placed in the public school libraries evokes the question whether that action might not be an unconstitutional attempt to "strangle the free mind at its source."

Id. at 190 (quoting *West Virginia State Bd. of Educ. v. Barnette,* 319 U.S. 624, 637, 87 L. Ed. 1628, 63 S. Ct. 1178 [1943]). The court also noted that the school board's failure to follow its own procedures raised suspicion that the motivation of the school board was unconstitutional. *Id.* at 190–91.

In the present case, the court must determine the "actual motivation" of the school board members in their removal decision. If the decisive factor behind the removal of *Annie on My Mind* was the school board members' personal disapproval of the ideas contained in the book, then under *Pico* the removal was unconstitutional.

The Board of Education members who voted in favor of the removal of *Annie on My Mind* stated that they believed the book was "educationally unsuitable." The court is required to assess the "credibility of [school officials'] justifications for their decision." *Pico,* 457 U.S. at 875.

There is no basis in the record to believe that these Board members meant by "educational suitability" anything other than their own disagreement with the ideas expressed in the book. Here, the invocation of "educational suitability" does nothing to counterbalance the overwhelming evidence of viewpoint discrimination.

Accordingly, the court concludes that defendants removed *Annie on My Mind* because they disagreed with ideas expressed in the book and that this factor was the substantial motivation in their removal decision. Through their removal of the book, defendants intended to deny students in the Olathe School District access to those ideas. Defendants unconstitutionally sought to "prescribe what shall be orthodox in politics, nationalism, religion, or other matters of opinion." *Pico,* 457 U.S. at 872; *West Virginia State Bd. of Educ. v. Barnette,* 319 U.S. 624, 642, 87 L. Ed. 1628, 63 S. Ct. 1178 (1942).

The highly irregular and erratic manner in which defendants removed *Annie on My Mind* from the District's libraries and their disregard of established policy and procedure are important evidence of their improper motivation. See *Pico,* 457 U.S. at 874–75; *Campbell,* 64 F.3d at 190–91. In addition, defendants did not consider or discuss less restrictive alternatives to complete removal of the book. This is also persuasive evidence of improper motivation. See *Campbell,* 64 F.3d at 190.

Defendants have argued that they have broad discretion to transmit community values, and that they may remove library books based upon their personal social, political, and moral views. The Supreme Court in *Pico* expressly rejected this argument, noting that "petitioners' reliance upon that duty [to transmit community values through curriculum]

is misplaced where, as here, they attempt to extend their claim of absolute discretion beyond the compulsory environment of the classroom, into the school library and the regime of voluntary inquiry that there hold sway." *Pico,* 457 U.S. at 869.

Defendants also have argued that plaintiffs have not been denied access to the book because it is available from sources outside of the school library. The availability of *Annie on My Mind* from other sources does not cure defendants' improper motivation for removing the book. "Restraint on expression may not generally be justified by the fact that there may be other times, places, or circumstances available for such expression." *Minarcini v. Strongsville City Sch. Dist.,* 541 F.2d 577, 582 (6th Cir. 1976) (removal of books because school board found them distasteful was unconstitutional).

In accordance with the analysis in *Pico* and *Campbell,* the court concludes that defendants' removal of *Annie on My Mind* from the Olathe School District libraries was a violation of plaintiffs' First Amendment rights. In addition, the Kansas Constitution, Bill of Rights § 11 entitles plaintiffs to prevail on their free speech claim to the same extent that they have prevailed on their First Amendment claim under the United States

Constitution. See *Unified Sch. Dist. No. 503 v. McKinney,* 236 Kan. 224, 234–35, 689 P.2d 860 (1984) (using United States Supreme Court decisions as persuasive authority in state free speech analysis); *State v. Russell,* 227 Kan. 897, 899, 610 P.2d 1122, cert. denied, 449 U.S. 983, 66 L. Ed. 2d 245, 101 S. Ct. 400 (1980) (federal and state free speech provisions generally considered coextensive).

Due Process Claim

The Fourteenth Amendment to the United States Constitution prohibits states from depriving "any person of life, liberty or property, without due process of law. . . ." U.S. Const. amend 14, § 1. Plaintiffs seek to establish that their due process rights were violated by the Olathe School District's failure to follow its own procedures. Although the court finds the District's failure to observe its own removal rules as evidence of an improper motive, the court does not agree that the failure to follow these procedures creates a constitutional due process violation. See *Bicknell v. Vergennes Union High Sch. Bd. of Directors,* 638 F.2d 438, 442 (2d Cir. 1980) (decided the same day as the Second Circuit's decision in *Pico v. Board of Educ.,* 638 F.2d 404 [2d Cir. 1980], aff'd, 457 U.S. 853, 73 L. Ed. 2d 435, 102 S. Ct. 2799 [1982]).

The court is not convinced that plaintiffs have a liberty or property interest in the removal of a book from the school library. See *id.* (deprivation resulting from the removal of a book from the school library is not a particularized and personal interest that would entitle student or librarian to a hearing prior to removal). With regard to procedural due process, defendants provided an opportunity for members of the public and plaintiffs to express their views at the January 1994 school board meeting. The public board meeting satisfied the minimum federal constitutional requirements. See *Cleveland Bd. of Educ. v. Loudermill,* 470 U.S. 532, 541, 84 L. Ed. 2d 494, 105 S. Ct. 1487 (1985). The court concludes that defendants' removal of *Annie on My Mind* did not violate plaintiffs' due process rights under the Fourteenth Amendment.

Conclusion

For the foregoing reasons, the court concludes that defendants' removal of *Annie on My Mind* from the Olathe School District libraries violated plaintiffs' constitutional rights under the First Amendment of the United States Constitution and under the Constitution of the State of Kansas, Bill of Rights, § 11. Further, the court concludes that defendants did not violate plaintiffs' due process rights under the Fourteenth Amendment.

The court orders defendants to return the copies of *Annie on My Mind* to the libraries in the Olathe School District where they were located prior to the removal. This is to be accomplished on or before January 2, 1996. The court further orders that the books be made available according to the usual terms and conditions prescribed for the use of library materials in the District.

Pursuant to 28 U.S.C. § 1988, plaintiffs are entitled to an award of attorneys fees, costs, and expenses associated with the prosecution of this case. Counsel are ordered to confer and attempt to reach an agreement regarding the fee award. See D. Kan. Rule 54.2.

It is so ordered.
G. T. Van Bebber
United States District Judge

Notes

1. A media specialist within the Olathe School District is the equivalent of a librarian.
2. Her educational views appear to comport with those of Thomas Gradgrind in *Hard Times,* by Charles Dickens.

Computerized Reading Programs

All elementary schools in the school district use Accelerated Reader (AR), and the library media specialists feel pressured to purchase books to accommodate the needs of students who read at middle and high school levels. Some school library media specialists use the AR book lists as a selection aid, but others have pointed out that some of the books on the AR advanced lists are not appropriate for elementary school students.

High-achieving students must be served, but reading level and maturity level are not the same. In most cases, a fifth-grade student who reads on the eleventh-grade reading level is not ready for the novels high school students read. It is important to note that AR is a company that sells a reading program to schools. It is not a book-selection tool. The reading levels assigned to the books on its lists are determined by a formula that measures readability only. Take a good look at the AR reading lists and note that *Beloved* by Toni Morrison is assigned a 6.0 reading level and *Lords of Discipline* by Pat Conroy a 6.6 reading level. School library media centers must have materials that challenge students to grow educationally and individually, but maturity level of students must be considered.

There are a variety of methods for developing an appropriate collection for gifted students, including these:

- Ask teachers of gifted students if they have reading lists appropriate for these students.
- Form a coalition of elementary library media specialists to make recommendations to one another.

- Talk with middle school media specialists and language arts teachers, and ask what books they would like students to read before coming to middle school.
- Get help from the school district's gifted coordinator or language arts coordinator.
- Note the age recommendation on book reviews.
- Consider the classics. For example, novels like *Little Women* and *The Jungle Book* have high reading levels because of the language patterns of the era in which they were written.
- Ask the students to recommend books for their peers. ■

Materials Selection Checklist

☐ Does the school district have a materials selection policy?

☐ Does the policy include nonprint materials?

☐ Is there a reconsideration policy for challenged materials?

☐ Are the faculty and administration aware of these policies?

☐ Do the faculty understand their rights and responsibilities to participate in materials selection?

☐ Do parents understand their children's rights to materials that serve their personal and educational needs?

☐ What is the library media center's responsibility toward providing materials for student-sponsored activities such as debate team or the school newspaper?

☐ What is the responsibility of the school to provide materials to English-language learners?

CHAPTER 2

Library Management and Programs

Libraries are not made; they grow.

Augustine Birrell

I f a school library media center is not careful, its collection management practices may begin to look like professional censorship. Well-developed policies that address all areas of collection management provide guidance for school library media specialists as they develop strategic plans for the growth of their school library media programs and services. Management policies should reflect the educational goals of the school community while promoting the principles of intellectual freedom. In this way, library media specialists are equipped to make objective decisions about the management

Questions to Consider When Evaluating a Collection

- Is the material in poor condition?
- How often has the material circulated?
- Is the content outdated?
- Does the material present a biased point of view?
- Does the material portray stereotypes?
- Is the material of poor quality?
- Are revised editions available?
- Does the material fit the overall selection guidelines in the school district's policy manual?
- Is the reading level of the material too easy or too difficult for most students in the school?

practices in their library media centers and avoid any misunderstanding of purpose or appearance of self-censorship. Such practices include evaluation of materials, organization of the collection, circulation policies, interlibrary loans, reserved materials, programs. The entire school population should have the highest expectations that the school library media center serves the educational and personal needs of all students and that materials and practices are evaluated yearly to accommodate necessary changes to meet such requirements.

CASE STUDY 1

Evaluating the Collection

A school library media specialist has overcrowded shelves and decides to evaluate the collection at the end of the school year when he takes inventory. In the past year, a neighboring school district has been challenged on books that deal with the occult. The news media have reported these challenges so much that the community is in an uproar about the "evil forces" that may affect and influence their children. The school library media specialist fears that these challenges could cause parents in his school to request the removal of similar books. He decides to scrutinize books dealing with the occult closely and to consider removing them from the collection. In this way, he may avoid a messy challenge like those that have occurred nearby. He does not think that this is censorship since he is removing them during the evaluation and weeding process.

Removing books on the occult, without due process, is indeed censorship, regardless of when it is done. This school library media specialist is attempting to put out a fire that may never be lit in his school. If parents wish to challenge such materials, then they should be asked to follow the process outlined in the school district's materials reconsideration policy. A collection should not be shaped because of fear of a potential challenge. A school library must have materials that appeal to all types of readers. Those students who wish to read books that deal with the occult should have them available.

Specific guidelines for evaluating a school library media center's collection should be included in the district's policy manual. Maintaining an accurate, relevant, and useful collection is important, and this can only occur when a school library media specialist has a systematic process for evaluating the collection. ∎

Evaluating Library Collections: An Interpretation of the Library Bill of Rights

The continuous review of library materials is necessary as a means of maintaining an active library collection of current interest to users. In the process, materials may be added and physically deteriorated or obsolete materials may be replaced or removed in accordance with the collection maintenance policy of a given library and the needs of the community it serves. Continued evaluation is closely related to the goals and responsibilities of each library and is a valuable tool of collection development. This procedure is not to be used as a convenient means to remove materials that might be viewed as controversial or objectionable. Such abuse of the evaluation function violates the principles of intellectual freedom as well as the Preamble and Articles I and II of the Library Bill of Rights, which state:

> The American Library Association affirms that all libraries are forums for information and ideas, and that the following basic policies should guide their services.
>
> I. Books and other library resources should be provided for the interest, information, and enlightenment of all people of the community the library serves. Materials should not be excluded because of the origin, background, or views of those contributing to their creation.
>
> II. Libraries should provide materials and information presenting all points of view on current and historical issues. Materials should not be proscribed or removed because of partisan or doctrinal disapproval.

The American Library Association opposes internal censorship and strongly urges that libraries adopt guidelines setting forth the positive purposes and principles of evaluation of materials in library collections.

Adopted February 2, 1973; amended July 1, 1981; July 2, 2008.

Organization of Materials: An Issue of Labeling

All elementary school library media centers in one district in the state are pressured to place books on the shelves by reading level so that students may easily locate the books of their appropriate level. This practice requires that library media specialists purchase stickers for all books and use shelf signage to indicate the reading level of the books at that particular location. The media specialists feel that this practice helps teachers guide their students to suitable reading materials and demonstrates a team effort in supporting the reading curriculum.

Although library media specialists are always willing to support teachers in serving the special needs of students, there is also a professional obligation to avoid violating students' rights for free access to the entire collection. A school library media specialist may determine the best way to organize the library media center's collection, but she should make sure that the organization of the collection is from a neutral viewpoint. In other words, any attempt to attach prejudicial labels to portions of the collection violates the principles of intellectual freedom and ultimately places unfair restrictions on library users. Reading-level stickers are prejudicial and should not be used to limit students' use of the library media center collection and services. Acceptable, unbiased organization and labeling of the collection may include designated areas for reference materials, special collections such as rare books, and paperback books.

Libraries do not remove labels that are affixed by a publisher, such as readability levels on beginning reader materials. These books, however, should be shelved with all other books so that students are free to select them without being judged by another patron. ∎

CASE STUDY 3

Labels on MARC Records

The school library media center's catalog may be accessed from the school's website. Some parents have requested that the reading level be placed on the MARC record of each book to guide them in directing their children to their appropriate reading levels in bookstores or at the public library. This is a lot of work for the library media specialist, and she feels that this practice of labeling reaches beyond her role as library media manager.

The library media specialist should avoid placing such labels on MARC records. If parents are determined to have this information, they may access the websites of Accelerated Reader or the computerized reading program used by their child's school. Parents are requesting such labels in response to a national and local focus on testing and improving reading scores. Media specialists should assure parents that they will work with their children to guide them toward books that interest them. Most children can read books they are interested in, and they should be allowed to do this without restriction. This issue can be dealt with by conducting a workshop with parents to help them understand the chilling effect such reading levels have on their children's development of a lifelong love of reading. A brief article on labeling for the school's newsletter or website may also help parents understand this issue. ∎

Conversation Overheard in Bookstore

Mom: Johnny needs a book on the third-grade reading level. Can you help me?

Bookstore owner: What does Johnny enjoy reading?

Mom: It doesn't matter as long as it is on the third-grade reading level.

Bookstore owner: Don't you think he has special interests?

Mom: At this point, he needs fifteen points. I don't really care. He just has to meet his reading goal.

Bookstore owner: Has Johnny asked his media specialist for help? Maybe she can guide him.

Mom: She just wants the students to read. She doesn't care about their levels. Otherwise, she would label the books in the card catalog, and we wouldn't be in this mess.

Bookstore owner: I think you are right that your son's media specialist wants him to read.

Components of a Circulation Policy

- **Statement Regarding Purpose of Policy**
  Why am I writing this policy?
  What do I want this policy to achieve?
- **Loan Periods**
  Are loan periods the same for all types of materials?
  What are the specific loan periods?
- **Renewal of Materials**
  How often may a user renew items?
  What is the process of renewal?
- **Overdue Materials**
  Will there be overdue notices?
  How often are overdue notices sent?
  How are the notices issued?
  Will patron privacy be respected?
  What are patron consequences of overdue materials?
- **Lost or Damaged Materials**
  Will patrons be billed for lost or damaged materials?
  Do bills present an economic barrier to patrons?
  What happens if a patron does not pay for lost or damaged materials?
- **Restriction of Library Privileges**
  Are patrons ever restricted from library use?
  What behaviors result in restriction?
  Who make the decision?
- **Confidentiality of Library Records**
  Are there state confidentiality laws for library patrons?
  What provisions does the library media center make to assure patrons that
  confidentiality laws are followed?

CASE STUDY 4

Circulation Policies

A middle school student is delinquent in returning library materials, and the library media specialist feels that the student should not be allowed to take out more materials until she has returned those that are overdue. This student has a science project that requires the use of library media resources, and the science teacher insists that the student be allowed to take the materials necessary to complete her project.

Every school library media center must have a circulation policy that promises students and teachers fair access to the collection. In this case, the student needs the materials to complete an assignment, and every effort should be made to accommodate her. This may involve allowing the student to take a specified number of materials for overnight or weekend use; making special arrangements for the student to use the materials in the media center before and after school; working with the teacher to allow the student to come to the media center during class; helping the student identify full-text articles from databases that may be printed; or photocopying the portions of the books the student needs.

The circulation policy of the school library media center should be posted on the school's website so that students, as well as their parents, understand their responsibility when borrowing library materials. This policy should also be reviewed with students during the library media center orientation at the beginning of the school year and should be reinforced when working with classes on special projects. Faculty must also know the circulation policy. They should expect the school library media specialist to work with students to assure them a rewarding and successful educational experience. ■

CASE STUDY 5

Interlibrary Loan

Fifth-grade students in all elementary schools in a district are required to construct a scrapbook on the history of a particular state. They are encouraged to choose the state of their birth. This scrapbook must include an illustrated narrative about the state bird, flower, tree and motto, song, geography, early history, settlers, Native American tribes, noteworthy personalities, universities and colleges, museums, libraries, theater groups, government, all of the former governors and their platforms, famous legislative acts, tourist's attractions, historic towns and monuments, and if possible interviews with contemporary state leaders.

Guidelines for Developing an Interlibrary Loan Policy

Definition of Interlibrary Loan: an agreement by which libraries agree to make materials available to each other.

Purpose of Interlibrary Loan: to provide wide access to materials needed for educational or personal use.

If either party violates the interlibrary loan policy, privileges may be suspended.

Scope of the Policy
- Rules regarding what materials are loaned to other libraries are determined by the lending library. Materials exempt from library loan may include rare books, fragile materials, resources in high demand in their own libraries, or reference books that normally do not circulate in the lending library.
- The lending library establishes the conditions of the loan, such as length of time borrowed, mailing costs, and duration of loan.

Compliance with Copyright Law: All libraries are expected to post and abide by U.S. copyright law.

Challenges to Materials: Such challenges should be handled in the same way as challenges to materials in the borrowing library.

Expenses: Libraries in an interlibrary loan agreement have the responsibility to lend materials without fee and to photocopy materials without fee within the guidelines of the copyright law. Should there be charges, the borrowing library is the responsible party.

Responsibility of Lending Library
- All decisions about the types of materials to be loaned are stated by the lending library.
- Loan periods should be reasonable.
- The lending library should honor all requests in a timely manner.
- Library ownership should be stamped on all materials loaned.
- The lending library should firmly state whether materials can be renewed.
- The lending library should expect all materials to be returned in good condition.
- A statement should be made that all materials are subject to recall.

Responsibility of Borrowing Library
- A school library media center should make it possible to provide materials in its own library that it now borrows if the demand indicates a significant current and future need of the materials.
- Member libraries have an obligation to make an effort to fulfill the requirements of the interlibrary loan agreement.
- The borrowing library must be in full compliance with the interlibrary loan agreement.
- Students and parents should be informed of interlibrary services.
- The borrowing library is responsible for the protection of the interlibrary loan materials. It may not permit these materials to circulate. If it does grant permission, the patron is fully responsible for the materials.
- Delivery methods should be established.

Method of Request
- Requests must be made through school library media staff.
- Proper forms must be completed.
- The library media specialist communicates the request through the channels outlined by the district.

This is a time-management assignment issued at the beginning of the first semester of school and due at the end of the semester. The problem is that the school library media center has only two books on each state, access to an online encyclopedia, and a subscription to one biographical database that provides thumbnail sketches and a few full-text articles on note-worthy personalities of the past. There is little information on contemporary personalities. The public library has expressed a concern that the demands for materials on these subjects seriously limit their ability to serve all of the fifth-grade students in the district. Borrowing from libraries in other schools and public libraries in the state or other parts of the country is a possibility, but the school district has traditionally discouraged interlibrary loan and does not have a policy for library media specialists to follow.

Interlibrary loan is essential to serving the information needs of students. It is not practical to own numerous books and materials on a specific subject that are in demand only one semester of the school year. Interlibrary loan is a way for school media centers to extend their collections, but it is not an alternative to good collection development. It is the best way to extend library services and make available the vast numbers of materials that students need to satisfy this extensive time-management assignment. The best place to start is to develop a relationship with other libraries along with policies that guide students who borrow materials through interlibrary loan. Some states have a school library cooperative. It may become a little more complicated to arrange loans through libraries in other states. This is where the public library can help. It is important to inform the public library staff of student needs so that they are prepared to deal with the huge demands on their materials and interlibrary loan services.

The school district should develop a policy and ask that all school libraries abide by it. ■

Reserved Materials

A high school teacher sponsors an after-school seminar on world religions. He places reading materials and several films on reserve in the library media center so that students interested in the seminar will come prepared with background information. One of the books that he places on reserve deals with Islam. A student who has had little time to use the materials asks that he be allowed to take this particular book home overnight. The library media specialist knows that this student's family practices a very conservative Christian religion. She fears that they will challenge the book if they know it is in the media center's collection.

Typically, school library media specialists place materials on reserve at a teacher's request so that all students who need them have access to them. The purpose of a reserve shelf is not to remove access or to avoid a challenge by limiting the materials' use. Instead, it is a practice to extend access to particular students for a short period of time. It is never appropriate to assume that a student's faith will cause him or his parent to lodge a challenge. Once the unit of study or special event is over, the materials should be taken off reserve and returned to the open library shelves. Since most school library media centers are closed at night and on weekends, it seems reasonable to allow students to check out the materials when the center is closed. There should be a stated policy regarding the circulation of reserved materials on the school's website. This policy should also be communicated to students during library orientation at the beginning of the school year. Encourage faculty members who place materials on reserve to include this statement of policy on their syllabus. ∎

Reserved Materials and Copyright

A high school American history teacher wants to make a connection between the music, art, and history of World War II. He asks the school's music and art teachers to help him identify works appropriate for the unit. The school's library media center does not have an extensive collection of art books or music CDs, so the history teacher has borrowed art books and music CDs from the public library and wants to make copies to put on reserve for his students. The school library media specialist feels that this is breaking copyright law. The teacher then asks that he be allowed to place the materials from the public library on reserve.

It is important that teachers understand copyright law and that the school library media center's reserve policy include a statement regarding copyright. Most educators have the mistaken notion that copying anything is permissible when it is for educational purposes. This is not the case, and it is the responsibility of the school library media specialist to communicate and enforce copyright law as it applies to school library media services.

Many schools have a policy about placing personal materials or materials from other libraries on reserve. If this practice is permitted, there should be a statement that releases the school library media center from any responsibility for lost materials. ■

Copyright: Photocopying and Digital Reproduction

In the Copyright Act of 1976 (U.S. Code, Title 17), Congress establishes "exclusive rights of copyright"—the right to reproduce copies, the right to distribute copies to the public, the right to create derivative works based on the original, and the rights to publicly perform or display a work—to authors, creators, and other rights holders as an incentive to create and make available creative works to the public. Congress allows that only the rights holder can exercise these activities, providing them with a statutory monopoly. However, Congress also creates limitations to the copyright monopoly to ensure that the law meets its purpose to "advance the progress of Science and the Useful Arts." These limitations include the public domain, the principle that original creative *expressions* of ideas can be protected by copyright but neither ideas themselves nor facts can be protected, as well as important exceptions for users of copyrighted works. In particular, the key role that educational institutions and libraries play in the advancement of learning is recognized in the law, and special exceptions are provided exclusively to them.

One important library exception is Section 108: "limitations on exclusive rights: reproductions for libraries and archives." This exception allows qualifying libraries and archives the right to make reproductions without authorization for preservation, replacement, and interlibrary loan and for other limited copying performed by the library for library users. All copies made must include a notice of copyright that appears on the work or a legend that states that the work may be protected by copyright. In addition, the law requires that libraries post copyright warning statements at public photocopiers and on interlibrary loan forms.

As you can tell, Section 108's focus is dominated by the use of photocopy technology. In fact, at the time the 1976 copyright law was being drafted, photocopiers were the newfangled technology that potentially threatened the economic interests of rights holders. Previously, no other technology could so easily make tangible copies for a relatively low cost.

Since the 1976 legislation, Congress has made several amendments to the law, including the Digital Millennium Copyright Act of 1998 and the Technology, Education, and Copyright Harmonization (TEACH) Act of 2002, to address advancements in digital technologies. Nevertheless, much of the copyright law does not specifically address how libraries should handle copying done for a variety of library services—for digital reference, for reserve services, for staff development, and so on. Although it is frustrating to many, this lack of specificity is desired in the law because it allows for unforeseen circumstances, situations, and the evolving nature of technology. Thus, the librarian's primary tool for determining whether copying or the use of another exclusive right of copyright is lawful is the Fair Use section (Section 107) of the copyright law.

Fair use is often called an "equitable rule of reason": given the particular situation at hand (e.g., can photocopies of articles be placed by reserve for students?), is it *fair* to exercise a right of copyright without prior authorization? Four factors are considered to determine if a use is fair:

1. Purpose of the use: Is the use for educational, nonprofit purposes or for commercial purposes?
2. Nature of the publication: Is the work being used a published or unpublished work? Is it an extremely

current work, such as a best-seller? Is it a highly creative work, such as a motion picture? Is it a primarily factual work, such as a journal article?

3. Amount of the publication used: Is a small portion copied? Is a key portion—"the heart of the work"—copied? Is the entire work copied?

4. Effect on the market for the work: Is the copying done to avoid purchasing a copy of the work in the marketplace? Does the copying interfere with new markets associated with the work?

These factors are the same factors that a court would consider when reviewing a copyright infringement case.

In case study 7, the fairness of placing photocopies of art books and music CDs borrowed from the public library on library reserve is questioned. A librarian can make an assessment of this situation by applying the four factors. The purpose of the use (factor 1) is nonprofit and educational, which tend to be fair compared to a use for commercial purposes (because rights holders have the exclusive right to "market" their work). The nature of the works (factor 2) in our scenario is highly creative—art books with high-quality photography and music CDs with musical compositions and performances involved. Highly creative works—versus works that are more factual in nature, such as newspaper articles or scholarly journal publications—are considered more valuable under the copyright law, and use of these works without authorization is more likely to be unfair. The amount (factor 3) of the work copied is the entire work, which also weighs against fair use. The effect on the market (factor 4) for work appears negative—one presumably could purchase copies of these works rather than make entire unauthorized copies. Considering these conditions, one can determine that copying these entire works for placement on reserve likely infringes copyright.

Placing the physical copies of the works themselves on reserve is a more reasonable solution because, not only making additional copies is not necessary, the physical copies (purchased by the public library) will have limited exposure to a select number of students. The public library loses access to its copies during the loan period, just as it would if the works were loaned to the students in turn. Placing the works themselves on reserve carves out a short period of time when the students can more likely access the works.

Suppose the American history teacher plans to use the same resources for his course on World War II next year? Continued use of the resources suggests that the school library purchase its own copies of the works for placement on reserve.

Additional Resources

Copyright Act of 1976 (U.S. Code, Title 17)

Copyright Advisory Network: http://librarycopyright.net

Fair Use Check List, Copyright Management Center, Indiana University/Purdue University in Indianapolis: www.copyright.iupui.edu/checklist.htm

United States Constitution, Article I, Section 8

Circulation Records of Reserved Materials

A teacher in a middle school has placed several materials on reserve. A student in her class has not completed the assignment that required the use of these materials. The school library uses a very simple circulation log of reserved materials, and the teacher has demanded to see the log. She has a conference scheduled with this student's father in which she intends to prove that the issue is poor time management, not access to the materials. The school library media specialist destroys the log at the end of each class period, but the teacher feels that it is the school library media specialist's role to help prove that the student has had access to the materials.

This is a privacy issue, and the school library media specialist is right to destroy the circulation log of these materials. The student is responsible for his assignment, and it is not the role of the school library media specialist to monitor any student's use of the reserved materials. It is advisable to develop a record-keeping system that automatically destroys such records. One very easy way to handle this situation is to suggest to the teacher that she communicate to the parent that the student has access to the materials before, during, and after school hours. Also, it is important that a parent know the policy regarding overnight use of reserved materials. The responsibility should be placed on the student to complete the assignment in the allotted time. The role of the library media specialist is to have firm but reasonable policies that allow access to the information needed. Such policies should reinforce but not monitor responsible time management. ∎

Confidentiality and Library Records

In a library (physical or virtual), the right to privacy is the right to open inquiry without having the subject of one's interest examined or scrutinized by others. Confidentiality exists when a library is in possession of personally identifiable information about users and keeps that information private on their behalf. ("Privacy: An Interpretation of the Library Bill of Rights")

Protecting reader privacy and confidentiality is an ethical and legal obligation for the library profession. The ALA Code of Ethics calls on librarians to protect each library user's right to privacy and confidentiality "with respect to information sought or received and resources consulted, borrowed, acquired or transmitted." State library confidentiality laws or attorneys' general opinions protect the confidentiality of library records in all fifty states and the District of Columbia. (See chapter 4 for a detailed discussion of state library privacy laws and the legal basis for protecting confidentiality in the library.)

The AASL Position Statement on the Confidentiality of Library Records recognizes these obligations and urges school library media specialists to respect the privacy rights of youth and children. Young people may not seek out needed information or may avoid using the library media center if they believe their reading and use of the library media center's resources are easily divulged to teachers, school personnel, or their parents.

Records that connect specific students with the use of specific resources, programs, or services should be kept confidential and released only in accordance with the law and the media center's privacy policy. The privacy policy should assure that the library media center's records are used only for the purposes for which they are created and are kept only for the time needed for efficient operation of the media center.

Additional Resources

ALA Code of Ethics: www.ala.org/ala/aboutala/offices/oif/statementspols/codeofethics/codeethics.cfm

AASL Position Statement on the Confidentiality of Library Records: www.ala.org/ala/mgrps/divs/aasl/aaslproftools/positionstatements/aaslpositionstatementconfidentiality.cfm

Privacy: An Interpretation of the Library Bill of Rights: www.ala.org/ala/aboutala/offices/oif/statementspols/statementsif/interpretations/privacy.cfm

State Privacy Laws regarding Library Records: www.ala.org/ala/aboutala/offices/oif/ifgroups/stateifcchairs/stateifcinaction/stateprivacy.cfm

Checklist for Determining Reserve Policy

1. What is the purpose of placing specific materials on reserve?
2. How long should the materials remain on reserve?
3. Who determines the materials to be placed on reserve?
4. Will the materials circulate overnight and on weekends when the library media center is not open?
5. Is there a statement about limitations under copyright law, especially as it applies to photocopied articles or library-made copies of music CDs?
6. Will personal materials or materials borrowed from other libraries be placed on reserve?
7. What happens with circulation records of reserved materials?

CASE STUDY 9

Book Fairs and Censorship

Elementary and middle schools have book fairs at least once a year. Some schools use commercial book fair companies such as Scholastic Book Fairs, which preselects books. Other schools use local bookstores to supply the books the library media specialist has selected. One parent complained that there were not enough book choices for her fifth-grade child. She expected to find all of the Newbery Medal winners and honor books. For some reason, these books were not offered, and she demanded to know why. Meanwhile, across town at a middle school, a parent complained that there were too many fantasy books that promoted "evil forces" in the school's book fair.

School book fairs should be managed in much the same way as a library media center book collection. A library media specialist should not be expected to endorse every book in the book fair collection. In the case of a commercial book fair company like Scholastic Book Fairs, the books are preselected by a dedicated staff of professionals who consider their customers' age range of interest. In most cases, a school library media specialist may request that certain titles be included in the book fair offerings. For example, if *Kira Kira* by Cynthia Kadohata is not in the preselected book fair collection for elementary schools, the library media specialist can request that the book be sent. Such companies cannot possibly meet the needs of all schools without the help of local library media specialists. They do not know the community, and they do not know the reading habits of the students in the particular schools they serve. They make their selections based on their knowledge of children in a wider community.

The complaint in the middle school should be dealt with in the same way a book challenge is handled. First, the media specialist should explain to the parent that the book fair, like the library media center, is about choice. The fantasy books were chosen because so many students in the middle grades read them and ask for them. The reason a library media center has a book fair is to put books in the hands of children. A successful book fair serves the reading tastes of all children. Try to reason with the parent and help her know that her child will be led to the books that interest him. If she does not want him to read fantasy books, then she needs to instruct him not to purchase them. ■

CASE STUDY 10

Banned Books Week

A high school library media center celebrates Banned Books Week by engaging the students in many different activities. There is a trivia contest about banned books, but the highlight of the week is an Open Microphone, held during lunch on the last day of the weeklong celebration. During this time, students and faculty read from their favorite banned book and share why the book was banned. A man in the community comes to campus and listens. Two days later, in a letter to the governor he writes that the school is wasting valuable time with such trivia. He actually poses the question "Why are students reading such junk and pornography?"

Banned Books Week has been celebrated in this country since 1982. The reason for this celebration is to promote free speech and the free exchange of ideas. Each September, school, public, and academic libraries celebrate this special event by offering

Sponsors of Banned Books Week

American Booksellers Association
American Booksellers Foundation for Free Expression
American Library Association
American Society of Journalists and Authors
Association of American Publishers
National Association of College Stores
Endorsed by the Center for the Book of the Library of Congress

Challenged Books and Student Responses

Dear Ms. Jones:

Thanks for talking to us about the First Amendment. I learned that people are censoring books because they are reading things into books that the author did not mean or intend. Or, they see words that have double meanings and automatically think that kids will think the worst. These people should not be allowed into libraries if all they do is limit our freedoms. I really appreciate the First Amendment because it allows us to do what we want to do and think, and not what somebody else wants us to do and think.

Sincerely,

Amy
[eighth grade]

Dear Mrs. Jones:

I recently read the article "Questions about *Shiloh*" in your newsletter. I began to think about the meaning of the book *Shiloh* by Phyllis Reynolds Naylor. Although this book consists of a terrible man named Judd Travers who abuses and kicks his dogs, curses, spits, and chews tobacco, it is proven in the book what a cruel man he is. I think that any child wouldn't want to be like this terrible man. I know I certainly don't! Therefore, I think Judd is an influence for children to grow up more like Marty, the loving main character, and less like Judd. What do you think? Do you think children want to grow up to be so dreadful?

Sincerely,

Jenny
[sixth grade]

a variety of programs that center around the freedom to read. Most library patrons, including students in public and private schools, are appalled at the titles that have been challenged in this nation and dismayed that anyone in a "free" country would attempt to abridge their freedom to read them.

The man who complained about the high school's open microphone obviously has a problem with public education and the curriculum students are taught. The library media specialist should take this opportunity to let the governor know, without being defensive, what an education the Banned Books Week celebration has been for the school community. Perhaps the students would like to write to the governor. They are quite capable of putting things into perspective, and it gives them an opportunity to do exactly what Banned Books Week promotes—express their opinions. ■

Library Management and Programs Checklist

- ❏ Does the school or school district have a policy for evaluating the collection?
- ❏ Is the policy clear to school administrators?
- ❏ Does the school have a clear statement regarding organization of library materials?
- ❏ What is the school library media center's reserve policy?
- ❏ Is the library media center's reserve policy clear to students and faculty?
- ❏ What is the library media center's policy regarding photocopied articles or burned music CDs?
- ❏ Does the school library media center have a circulation policy?
- ❏ What is the school library media center's policy regarding overdue materials?
- ❏ Do all of the management policies of the school library media center promote free and fair access to the collection, services, and programs?

CHAPTER 3

Library Access

Nothing sickens me more than the closed door of a library.

Barbara Tuchman

A school library media center that is closed to its students serves no purpose at all. Students should have access to the entire collection; they should expect to use the collection without fear that their individual needs are being judged or monitored; they should have reasonable access to materials and services before, during, and after school hours; they should count on services that extend their learning and information needs without restriction of any type. A completely open door policy promotes an intellectually free environment and guarantees students and the entire school community a library media program that supports the overall missions of the school and school district.

Schools and school boards should make policies that address access issues specifically related to services and practices of the school library media program. Such policies should address restricted shelves, use of facilities, and the rights of all students to access the materials they need. There may be access questions unique to a specific school. In this case, it is likely that the school board would mandate a set of guidelines developed at the school level. Such issues may include classroom collections of library materials and student behavioral standards.

School board policies or guidelines for the library media center's use should be subject to yearly evaluation so that new guidelines are developed as needed to accommodate the learning resource needs of all students. The policies should be inclusive rather than exclusive, and students and parents should be aware of students' rights to free and unrestricted access to all of the materials in the school library media center.

CASE STUDY 1

Restricted Shelves

An elementary school has had several complaints about J. K. Rowling's Harry Potter books. The principal and the school library media specialist decide to put the books on a restricted shelf and require that students bring a note from their parents before they are permitted to take out these books. They do not believe that this is an act of censorship, because the school library media center has the books available to those who are allowed to read them.

Because restricted materials often deal with controversial, unusual, or "sensitive" subjects, having to ask a librarian or circulation clerk for access to them may be embarrassing or inhibiting for patrons desiring the materials. . . . Because restricted materials often feature information that some library patrons consider "objectionable," the potential user may be predisposed to think of the materials as "objectionable" and, therefore, be reluctant to ask for access to them.

"Restricted Access to Library Materials: An Interpretation of the Library Bill of Rights," *Intellectual Freedom Manual,* 6th ed., p. 176

The courts have already resolved this issue in *Counts v. Cedarville School District.* If all books that might be challenged were placed on restricted shelves, there would be no free access to materials in a school library media center. Requiring a note from a parent is placing a prejudicial label on materials and on the child who takes them out. In the Arkansas case, the parents felt that their child was labeled "evil" because they allowed her to read Harry Potter books.

The issue of restricted shelves may also come up when dealing with sex education materials like the award-winning books *It's Perfectly Normal, It's Not the Stork,* and *It's So Amazing* by Robie H. Harris and illustrated by Michael Emberley. Many school library media centers do not own the books, and if they do they are likely to place them in the professional collection or the nurse's office. Even public libraries sometimes place these books in the adult section so that parents have to check the books out for their children.

Is this not a form of restriction? The books were written for children and answer many of the questions that children have about sex. What if a child has a question that he is too embarrassed to ask an adult? Suppose a child is being sexually abused? Could a child approaching puberty want the comfort of knowing that her questions are normal? A child's "need to know" should be so important to a library media specialist that she includes the books in the school library media center's collection regardless of the potential controversy. There are many ways of restricting materials. Setting aside a special shelf that requires a note from a parent and limits a child's use of materials below or above his reading level and moving material to a professional or adult collection are some of the most blatant access issues that school library media center's deal with on a daily basis. ■

Tip

Robert asks the library media specialist for a Harry Potter book. Anthony says, "My mother doesn't want me to read those books. They are evil." A good response from the media specialist is, "That's fine Anthony, but Robert's mother wants him to read the books." By giving this type of response, the library media specialist has just demonstrated the principles of intellectual freedom to both students.

Counts v. Cedarville School District— Restricted Access in the School Library

In 2001, a parent in the Cedarville, Arkansas, school district filed a formal challenge to J. K. Rowling's *Harry Potter and the Sorcerer's Stone.* She claimed the book promoted witchcraft, the occult, and disrespect for adult authority. She asked the Cedarville school board to remove all the Harry Potter books from the district's school library media centers.

Pursuant to district policy, the district's library committee, composed of parents, teachers, librarians, students, and school administrators, reviewed *Harry Potter and the Sorcerer's Stone.* The committee voted unanimously to keep the series in the district's school media centers without any restrictions.

Despite the committee's recommendation, the school board voted 3-2 to limit students' access to the Harry Potter books because the books "taught witchcraft" and "might promote disobedience and disrespect for authority." As a result, the Harry Potter books were placed on a restricted shelf in the school library. Students wishing to read the books were required to present a signed permission slip from their parent or guardian.

Two parents sued the school district on behalf of their daughter, a student in the Cedarville schools. They argued that the restrictions violated their daughter's First Amendment right to access books freely in the school media center.

The federal district court agreed. In its opinion, *Counts v. Cedarville School District,* it held that the requirement that students have parental permission to read the Harry Potter books was an unconstitutional content-based restriction on students' right to access to information.

The court found that the school board's requirements attached a stigma to reading the Harry Potter books. It also found that the need to seek out a library media specialist and ask permission to see the books placed an undue burden on the student's First Amendment right to read and use materials in the library.

The court rejected the school board's argument that the student's rights could not be violated because she retained "unfettered access" to the books at home and at school (her parents signed a permission slip allowing her to check out Harry Potter books). It ruled that even minimal infringements on a student's ability to access books in the school library constituted a serious violation of First Amendment rights that could not be excused on the grounds that the student could access the books in other places.

According to the court, the restrictions could not be justified on the grounds that the books promoted disobedience and disrespect for adult authority:

> There is no evidence that any of the three Board members was aware of any actual disobedience or disrespect that had flowed from a reading of the Harry Potter books. Their concerns are, therefore, speculative. Such speculative apprehensions of possible disturbance are not sufficient to jus-

tify the extreme sanction of restricting the free exercise of First Amendment rights in a public school library.

Nor could the restrictions be justified by the board members' belief that the books promoted witchcraft as a religion or their fear that students would begin to practice witchcraft:

> Regardless of the personal distaste with which these individuals regard "witchcraft," it is not properly within their power and authority as members of defendant's school board to prevent the students at Cedarville from reading about it. As the Supreme Court said in *Pico,* our Constitution does not permit the official suppression of *ideas.*

The court enjoined the enforcement of the school board's restrictions and ordered the school board to return the Harry Potter books to the open shelves of the school library without any restrictions.

The decision in the *Counts* case demonstrates that a decision to limit access to a book in the library media center may violate the First Amendment if the intent is to prevent students from reading or viewing disfavored ideas or opinions. Such restrictions will be subject to strict review by the courts. Library media specialists should be cautious about imposing any restriction on students' access that interferes with the ability freely to read or use materials available in the library media center.

Additional Resources

Counts v. Cedarville School District, 295 F. Supp. 2d 996 (W.D. Ark. 2003)

Board of Education, Island Trees Union Free School District No. 26, v. Pico, 457 U.S. 853 (1982)

Restricted Shelves for Students with Special Needs

Joey is in a self-contained EH (emotionally handicapped) class. He comes to the media center often, but one day he cannot find the book he wants. He is leaving when the media specialist calls to him to let him know that the book is on the cart of books to be shelved. The media specialist approaches him with the book and notices that he is shaking. She asks the teacher about Joey and is told that he is terrified of a raised voice from an adult. This is helpful information for the media specialist, who can now deal more effectively with Joey.

A middle school has an extensive special education department. Some of the students are mainstreamed, but most are in self-contained classrooms. The special education teachers want specific shelves in the library media center for their students. The library media specialist understands their needs but does not think providing a specific shelf for them is the answer.

Special education students have a right to use all materials in the media center. The concerns of the special education teachers are well intended, but these students are already isolated enough. A better solution is to plan with the special education teachers, so that a professional is available to help these students when they come to the media center. Mainstreamed students may have very different needs from those in self-contained classrooms. These students may need something for a science project or a social studies unit. Just because they are mainstreamed special education students does not mean that they are not good readers.

It may be appropriate for the library media specialist to attend the conference for students' Section 504 plans (see below). Typically all personnel who work with special education students should have access to students' IEPs (individual education programs). This type of information is very helpful for a media specialist, who can learn exactly what the special needs are and whether there are behavioral issues as well.

Another approach in dealing with special education students is for the media specialist to plan short programs in the media center especially for them. Perhaps it is a read-aloud session, a simple research project that helps them learn to navigate the Internet and databases, or a chance for them to talk about books they like. These sessions should include the teacher and the special education aide, so that there are more adults who can give these students individual attention and make their time in the media center successful. ■

CASE STUDY 3

Reading Level: An Access Issue

Amy is in the fifth grade and wants to read The Secret Garden *by Frances Hodges Burnett, but her teacher and library media specialist tell her that she cannot read that book because it is beneath her level. They direct her to a group of books and tell her that these are the books from which she can select. Amy insists that she wants to read* The Secret Garden. *Finally, Amy's mother complains that her child should be allowed to read anything in the library she wants.*

Amy's mother is correct. Her daughter should have access to the entire collection and should not feel judged because she wants to read something that her teacher feels is beneath her reading level. Any student should be free to explore and use the entire library media collection. This may mean that a student like Amy selects something less challenging, or that other students take things beyond their ability. But a library media center should be the one place in the school where students are treated as

Positive Approach to a Simple Problem

Katie: I want a book about animals.

Media specialist: I bet you want a book with lots of pictures.

Katie: Yes.

Media specialist (knowing that Katie always returns books without their covers): I know exactly the kind of animal book you want. You like the books without covers.

Katie: Yes, Yes, Yes.

Services to Students with Disabilities

Under federal law, each child with a disability is guaranteed a free and appropriate public education designed to meet his or her needs. This right is assured by two different but complementary laws.

The Individuals with Disabilities Education Act (IDEA) requires schools to *provide special education and related services* that are necessary to assure the students' academic success and future independent living. These programs and services are provided in addition to the programs available to students without disabilities and are remedial in nature. Students with specific disabilities such as autism, learning disabilities, hearing, speech and language impairments, mental disabilities, traumatic brain injury, and visual impairment are eligible to receive services under IDEA.

Section 504 of the Rehabilitation Act of 1973 prohibits *discrimination against individuals with disabilities.* Section 504 requires schools to "level the playing field" to eliminate barriers to full participation by students with disabilities. Section 504 is intended to assure equal access to the school's programs and facilities and is available to any student who needs an accommodation to participate in school activities on an equal basis with nondisabled students.

Both laws require that a school's faculty, staff, and administration work cooperatively with the student and the student's parents to develop a program that meets the student's unique needs. IDEA mandates the development of a specific "individual educational program," or IEP; Section 504 requires a less formal process but still requires schools to develop a "504 plan" to address a student's unmet needs. As resource specialists, library media specialists may be asked to participate and help design needed services and accommodations for a particular student.

Additional Resources

Individuals with Disabilities Education Act, 20 U.S.C. § 1400
Section 504 of the Rehabilitation Act of 1973, 29 U.S.C. § 794

individuals, without labels attached to their names or restrictions enforced because of such labels.

Amy's teacher and library media specialist want her to progress as a reader, but denying her access to the books that she wants to read may have a negative impact and actually turn her away from reading. Students are never too old or too smart to reread old favorites. Reading level should not keep them from enjoying such a process. ■

Toward the end of her third year, Shirley said to her library media specialist, "I wish I had a whole day to come to the library and read all the books I read in first, second, and third grades. Next year I will be too old." Think about an appropriate response to Shirley.

CASE STUDY 4

Facility Use

A high school library is closed for testing or other scheduled events, such as district principals' meetings, five days of every month. Students who need materials complain that they cannot use the library media center when they need it. Many of these meetings occur during lunch or immediately after school, when students want to use the facility. Most of the time the school library media center is open a half hour before and a half hour after regular school hours. Students and parents do not understand why the library media center is closed so much, and they request that students be allowed to use the center even if a meeting is in session. They also want longer library media center hours.

This is another common access issue, and one that should be addressed with the school's administration. In the event that this practice is completely out of hand, it is appropriate to ask the school board to adopt a policy that states that a school library media center must be open to students before, after, and during school hours when school is in session. Many accrediting agencies and associations require that a school library media center be open a specific amount of time before and after school. It should be assumed that the center is available to students during the school day. The practice of using a school library media center's space for testing is reasonable if the entire school is involved in testing; in this case, no student is denied access because all are required to participate in the testing program.

Administrators sometimes enjoy hosting meetings in their school. If the school does not have an auditorium or other large facility to accommodate the numbers of people attending the meetings, then the library media center is a logical place to use. Most of the time it does not occur to administrators that closing the media center doors to students during this time is denying them access to the resources and services of the media center. Media specialists should work with the administration and ask that they consider limiting their invitations to host such meetings to once or twice yearly. A few events like this do not have a negative impact on students for the long term. After-school meetings might be planned for after normal library hours.

Transportation and security issues may have a bearing on longer library hours; it depends upon the size and location of the school. Even the floor plan of the school may impact library hours: library media centers with outside doors may enjoy longer hours, since the rest of the school need not be open. Large schools that have several media specialists may offer longer hours because professionals can stagger work hours. Perhaps longer hours are necessary only when term papers are due or during exams when students need a quiet place to study.

These are all access issues that should be resolved at the beginning of the school year and evaluated at the end of the school year. Flexibility and a willingness to offer creative solutions to access issues are necessary if students are to have fair and free access to the library media center and its services. ■

Classroom Collections

A seventh-grade social studies teacher never wants her students to come to the library media center. She prefers to check out the books and materials that they need for their projects and house them in her classroom. In this way, she does not have to worry about students from other classes using the materials or bothering her students while they work. Since she wants to take the books out in her name, she does not feel that she should allow the students to take the books home. Who would be responsible for the materials if they were lost? Other social studies teachers complain because they are teaching the same unit and need materials to be available for their students as well.

This is a very real problem in schools and could arise on numerous occasions. It is unfair to allow one teacher to monopolize a specific portion of the collection by taking these items to the classroom, and such conduct should be viewed by other students and teachers as a direct denial of access to materials. Teachers are sometimes so focused on their own students' needs that they cannot see the needs of the entire school community. In an ideal situation, social studies teachers could stagger their units so that students might not all need the same materials at the same time. If they do, then the library media specialist should suggest placing the materials on reserve so that all students have access to them.

It is not likely that a school board would make a policy that deals with an issue this specific. It would more likely have a policy that states that all students should have access to the library media center and its materials. A school should set more detailed guidelines that are aligned with the broader school board policy. A committee made up of the library media specialist, students, parents, and faculty might be charged with setting explicit procedures for media center use.

Ask these questions when setting up procedures:

- How many classes may occupy the library media center in one given period?
- Is there a sign-up procedure for class use?
- How many individual students may use the facility without teacher supervision?
- What planning procedures are followed by teachers and media specialist so that students have optimum access to the facility and materials?
- Is there a copy of the teachers' syllabi on file in the media center so that the professional staff know exactly what is expected of students?
- What conditions warrant a teacher's need to maintain a classroom collection of library media materials? Are the guidelines flexible? ∎

Student Behavior and Denial of Access

Randy loves the library media center. He comes in every day before and after school and often uses the facility with his class. He does not have a computer at home, and he races to beat his classmates to the computers in the media center. Along the way, he jumps the furniture, creating a circus-like atmosphere in the media center. The assistant principal tells Randy that he cannot use the computers any longer if he has to jump the furniture to get to them. Randy's behavior does not stop, and the assistant principal bans him from the library media center for a month. He even tells Randy that he will have to sit in his office when Randy's class is using the media center.

There should be behavioral standards that all students are expected to follow, but banning Randy from the media center is not the answer. Since he does not have access to a computer at home, Randy is set up for failure when he is denied access to resources. A better way to deal with Randy is to arrange a contract with him. When he has an assignment due, guarantee him a certain amount of computer time a day. This may be before or after school or during lunch. He may also be granted a certain amount of time to complete an assignment while under the supervision of a teacher. It is possible that Randy's real problem is time management, and this is something that can be easily solved.

Students should be involved in setting the standards for student behavior in the media center. They are often stricter with their behavioral guidelines than the adults

Access to Resources and Services in the School Library Media Program: An Interpretation of the Library Bill of Rights

The school library media program plays a unique role in promoting intellectual freedom. It serves as a point of voluntary access to information and ideas and as a learning laboratory for students as they acquire critical thinking and problem-solving skills needed in a pluralistic society. Although the educational level and program of the school necessarily shape the resources and services of a school library media program, the principles of the Library Bill of Rights apply equally to all libraries, including school library media programs. Under these principles, all students have equitable access to library facilities, resources, and instructional programs.

School library media specialists assume a leadership role in promoting the principles of intellectual freedom within the school by providing resources and services that create and sustain an atmosphere of free inquiry. School library media specialists work closely with teachers to integrate instructional activities in classroom units designed to equip students to locate, evaluate, and use a broad range of ideas effectively. Intellectual freedom is fostered by educating students in the use of critical thinking skills to empower them to pursue free inquiry responsibly and independently. Through resources, programming, and educational processes, students and teachers experience the free and robust debate characteristic of a democratic society.

School library media specialists cooperate with other individuals in building collections of resources that meet the needs as well as the developmental and maturity levels of students. These collections provide resources that support the mission of the school district and are consistent with its philosophy, goals, and objectives. Resources in school library media collections are an integral component of the curriculum and represent diverse points of view on both current and historical issues. These resources include materials that support the intellectual growth, personal development, individual interests, and recreational needs of students.

While English is, by history and tradition, the customary language of the United States, the languages in use in any given community may vary. Schools serving communities in which other languages are used make efforts to accommodate the needs of students for whom English is a second language. To support these efforts, and to ensure equitable access to resources and services, the school library media program provides resources that reflect the linguistic pluralism of the community.

Members of the school community involved in the collection development process employ educational criteria to select resources unfettered by their personal, political, social, or religious views. Students and educators served by the school library media program have access to resources and services free of constraints resulting from personal, partisan, or doctrinal disapproval. School library media specialists resist efforts by individuals or groups to define what is appropriate for all students or teachers to read, view, hear, or access via electronic means.

Major barriers between students and resources include but are not limited to imposing age, grade-level, or reading-level restrictions on the use of resources; limiting the use of interlibrary loan and access to electronic information; charging fees for information in specific formats; requiring permission from parents or teachers; establishing restricted shelves or closed collections; and labeling. Policies, procedures, and rules related to the use of resources and services support free and open access to information.

It is the responsibility of the governing board to adopt policies that guarantee students access to a broad range of ideas. These include policies on collection development and procedures for the review of resources about which concerns have been raised. Such policies, developed by persons in the school community, provide for a timely and fair hearing and assure that procedures are applied equitably to all expressions of concern. It is the responsibility of school library media specialists to implement district policies and procedures in the school to ensure equitable access to resources and services for all students.

Adopted July 2, 1986, by the ALA Council; amended January 10, 1990; July 12, 2000; January 19, 2005; July 2, 2008.

in the school community. Make sure they understand issues related to access and ask them to consider these questions:

- What are reasonable behaviors for students in the media center?
- What consequences should be enforced if students disobey the rules?
- Should there be a time when a student is banned from the media center?
- What alternative forms of access should be available to students who are being punished? ■

CASE STUDY 7

Economic Barriers

Susan is a high school senior and needs materials for an English paper. She is not allowed to take out materials from the media center because she lost materials last year and never paid for them. The library media specialist told Susan that she would have to get her materials from the public library. Susan does not have transportation to the public library and she owes money for lost items there as well. She is going to fail the class if she does not write this paper.

This is a clear example of a rule that imposes an economic barrier on a user. Most schools do expect students to pay for lost materials, but there is not much a school can do to enforce it. If students do not have the money to pay for the items, then an arrangement should be made to get them the materials they need. It is in Susan's best interest to be a responsible library media center user, but she cannot be expected to pay for the materials if she does not have the money. Special arrangements should be made with Susan to pay her debt. Perhaps she is allowed to do small jobs before or after school in the media center. Help her organize her time so that she can use small periods of time in the media center to take notes. If Susan is successful, she is more likely to be a responsible user of the media center.

Library media specialists should know their district's board policy regarding imposing economic barriers on students. Some school board policies state that student debts may not carry over to the next school year. Others may allow it. Regardless of the policy, it is important to work with students to help them accept responsibility for media center materials, but at the same time let them know that their access to materials will never be denied. ∎

Library Access Checklist

- ❏ What is the law on restricted shelves?
- ❏ How does this law apply to students with special needs?
- ❏ What are the inclusion laws pertaining to students with special needs and library access?

- ❏ How is restricting a child by reading level an access issue?
- ❏ Is there a school board policy that deals with restricted access to the school library media facility?

- ❏ What is the school board policy about imposing an economic barrier on students' use of the media center and its materials?
- ❏ Are there school guidelines regarding acceptable student behavior in the media center?

CHAPTER 4

Labeling and Privacy

I don't read as good as a lot of people in my class. I just wish they didn't know that.

Eighth-grade student

There was a time when students had very little privacy in schools. Grades were frequently posted outside classroom doors, assignments marked in red were pinned to bulletin boards, and students' overdue library notices were posted so that the entire school community knew exactly what materials they had checked out. Students lived in fear of their "permanent records" and believed that the slightest recorded flaw would track them for life. It did not matter whether these records actually followed students past high school graduation; it was still a daunting

FOCUS

Library Confidentiality Statutes

Forty-eight states and the District of Columbia have adopted laws that specifically recognize the confidentiality of library records. Two states, Kentucky and Hawaii, do not have library confidentiality laws; instead, each state's attorney general has issued a binding opinion declaring library records confidential.

The requirements of these laws vary from state to state. At a minimum, each statute declares that library circulation records are confidential records not subject to disclosure under the state's open records law or freedom of information act. Many states extend additional protection to library records by imposing a duty on the library to protect user records from disclosure and limiting the circumstances under which a library may release records to third parties or law enforcement officers. For example, many state library confidentiality laws require a court order before a library can disclose records to law enforcement officers. A few state statutes make it a crime to disclose library records in a manner contrary to the law.

Library confidentiality laws may not apply to every library in a state, and they may create exceptions to the law for some library users. For example, some state library confidentiality statutes do not apply to private libraries, K–12 library media centers, or academic libraries. A few state laws contain exceptions that permit parents of minor children to examine their children's library records. Many states, however, choose to protect the confidentiality of all library users' records, without regard to the library user's age or the funding, ownership, or control of the library.

Every library media specialist should be familiar with the state's library confidentiality law and understand when it governs access to library records. If a state's library confidentiality statute applies to the records kept by the library media center, the law's requirements should be incorporated into the school's policies. For private schools and public schools not covered by a state's library confidentiality law, such laws can serve as public policy exemplars that provide a rationale and a basis for the institu-

tions' own policies protecting the confidentiality of student library records.

Additional Resource

State Privacy Laws regarding Library Records: www.ala.org/ala/aboutala/offices/oif/ifgroups/stateifcchairs/stateifcinaction/stateprivacy.cfm

feeling to know that a teacher, library media specialist, principal, and other school personnel could easily access, often from memory, students' grades, disciplinary records, and materials checked out of the library media center.

Of course, there must be records of student progress, and even serious disciplinary actions, but today's students enjoy a bit more privacy in school than did earlier generations. For example, not too many years ago social security numbers were used on all student records—name tags, academic records, library cards, cafeteria tickets, and disciplinary records. Then groups such as the American Student Government Association lobbied school districts and lawmakers about their concerns regarding privacy and the use of social security numbers. Now, it is illegal to use students' social security numbers as a unified means of identification in schools.

Some educators and library media specialists may question how much privacy a student should expect. This can best be answered by the school district's attorney. Privacy laws vary by state. Some states grant complete privacy of library records, which means that even parents cannot obtain information regarding their child's use of the library media center and its materials. Other states may have more limited privacy laws that allow parents full access to their children's library transactions. Regardless of the state law, it is in the best interest of students to grant them privacy in the library media center setting. Teachers often want to know what their students are reading, or the materials they are using, but it is never appropriate for the library media specialist to share this information. This is a conversation that should take place between the teacher and student.

Students use the library media center for many reasons. Whether they are looking for a good book to read or information to complete a school assignment, their recreational reading and information needs should be kept private unless they choose to reveal them. It is important for students to know that the library media specialist and staff support and respect their privacy. Maybe a student wants to whisper the information she needs; maybe he wants to search the computer alone; maybe she simply wishes to browse the shelves. It does not matter what students' purposes are for using the media center. It only matters that they are using it.

Labeling is a practice that is closely related to privacy. Students should have the freedom to use the media center and its entire collection without fear that they are being labeled in any way. Reading-level labels are perhaps the most common form of labeling in schools. These levels are often determined by companies such as Accelerated Reader or Lexile Framework for Reading, which use a scientific formula to assign the reading levels. Maturity level is completely disregarded by such labels, but it is an important factor in materials selection.

Another blatant form of labeling in school library media centers is content labeling of materials. An example is the Harry Potter case in Arkansas, discussed in chapter 3. The Harry Potter books were labeled "evil" by a segment of the population in Cedarville, Arkansas, so the books were placed on a restricted shelf, and parental permission was required before students could borrow them. The court ruled that requiring parental permission "labels" students, that such labeling is inappropriate, and that the books must be available to all students.

There is an ongoing debate among school library media specialists about issues related to labeling. Prejudicial content labeling is illegal, and media specialists must comply with the courts. Affixing reading-level labels to books and using these labels to deny students access to library media materials may not be illegal, but it is certainly

FOCUS

Family Educational Rights and Privacy Act

The Family Educational Rights and Privacy Act, 20 U.S.C. § 1232g (FERPA), controls disclosure of a student's educational records and information. It requires educational institutions to adopt policies that permit parents and students to inspect and correct a student's educational records. It also prohibits disclosure of a student's records without the written permission of the parents, or of the student if the student is age eighteen or older.

The Family Policy Compliance Office (FPCO), a part of the U.S. Department of Education, is the federal office charged with overseeing and enforcing FERPA. It frequently offers guidance and technical assistance to educational institutions by providing information on the law's application to particular circumstances.

Any record maintained by an educational institution directly related to a student, in any format, that allows the student to be identified from the information contained in it is considered an "educational record" by the FPCO. Analysts within the FPCO have issued guidance stating that library circula-

tion records and similar records maintained by a library media center are "educational records" under FERPA.

Though FERPA generally requires institutions to protect the privacy of educational records, it contains many exceptions that allow disclosure of a student's educational records without the consent of the student or parent. For example, FERPA permits educational institutions to release information contained in a student's records to any school official who has a "legitimate educational interest" in the records; to appropriate public officials in health and safety emergencies; and to courts and law enforcement agencies in response to a judicial order or lawfully issued subpoena. FERPA also permits educational institutions to disclose information about international students to the Department of Homeland Security and the Immigration and Customs Enforcement Bureau. In addition, colleges and universities may disclose records and information to the parents of adult students if the student is a tax dependent or is under age twenty-one and has violated any law

or regulation concerning the illegal use of drugs or alcohol.

FERPA thus *permits* disclosure of school library records when state library confidentiality statutes and professional ethics would otherwise prohibit such disclosure. FERPA, however, *does not require* the institution to disclose records under these circumstances, nor does FERPA require institutions to create or maintain particular records. Schools and library media centers may therefore craft policies that extend additional privacy protection to students' library records; adopt record retention policies that protect students' confidentiality in regard to their use of the library media center; and, where applicable, incorporate state law protections for library records.

Additional Resources

Code of Federal Regulations, Family educational rights and privacy, 34 C.F.R. Part 99

Family Educational Rights and Privacy Act, 20 U.S.C. 1232g

Family Policy Compliance Office, U.S. Department of Education: www.ed.gov/policy/gen/guid/fpco/index.html

an ethical issue. Children should have the opportunity to use the library and all of its materials. This cannot be accomplished if a student is relegated to one small section of the library media center.

There should be no prejudicial labels placed on any book selected for the media center. These levels can be devastating to a student and actually interfere with the learning process. Students' characters or their reading abilities should not be judged on the basis of what they are reading or the information they are seeking. There must, therefore, be a concerted effort by all members of the library media staff to keep students' reading choices private. This is why privacy laws and policies are so important to school library media center services and practices.

Reading-Level Labels

Mrs. Brown, a fifth-grade teacher, comes into the media center with Susan in tow. She expresses her concern that Susan has checked out a "baby" book and insists that she exchange the book for something on her reading level. The media specialist notices that Susan is withdrawing as Mrs. Brown talks.

Mrs. Brown has just done an excellent job of embarrassing Susan by exposing her reading choice. It is now up to the media specialist to help Susan overcome the humiliation of the moment. The media specialist might say to Susan, "That is a very good book that you have chosen. Enjoy reading it, but let me help you find another book so that you have plenty to read over the weekend. I know that you never like to be without a good book to read. You are one of my best readers." The media specialist has just restored Susan's dignity.

At a later time, the media specialist and Mrs. Brown should have a conversation about respecting students' privacy in the media center. There is a good chance that Mrs. Brown will not understand why labeling students by reading level is bad practice, and there is even a greater chance that she does not believe that students have rights of privacy. Use the following scenarios to help Mrs. Brown understand labeling:

- Mary is in fourth grade and reads at the tenth-grade reading level. Her friend Debbie reads at the fifth-grade reading level. Mary boasts that she can choose books from the bookshelf that houses higher-level reading materials, but Debbie has to choose baby books. Why should Mary know Debbie's reading level? What does this type of competition do to the self-esteem of either child?

- Ann is ten years old and wants to read *Are You There God? It's Me, Margaret* by Judy Blume. She reads at the adult level, is approaching puberty, and has questions similar to the ones Margaret asks in Blume's novel. Mrs. Grant, her teacher, notices that Ann is about to check out Blume's book. She tells her that she has to put the book back because it is labeled third-grade reading level. How does this affect Ann? Should she not be allowed to read at her emotional and maturity level? Why does everything she reads have to be at her reading level?

- John is in the fourth grade but reads at the first-grade reading level. He goes to the library media center with a note from his teacher: "John would like a book about military weapons, but he is a very poor reader. I doubt that there is anything in the collection on this subject that he can read. Please direct him to reading materials on his level." Why does John have to bring a note from the teacher? Should he not have the opportunity to tell the media specialist about his special interest? Has anyone considered that John's keen interest in military weapons may actually boost his reading level? What about the pictures? There is much knowledge to be gained from those.

- Quint is a third-grader and wants to take out *The Lion, the Witch, and the Wardrobe* by C. S. Lewis. Mr. Jones, his teacher, feels that the book is much beyond his reading ability and thinks that he should wait until he is in fifth grade to read the book. Quint insists that he wants the book and brings a note from his mother that demands that he be allowed to take the book. Mr. Jones writes the mother a note and explains that the book is not on Quint's reading

Reading Level Q&A

Q: How do I help a student who is obviously selecting books below his reading level?

A: The student should take the book he has chosen, but tell him about a more challenging title with a similar theme or subject. There is a good chance that the student will respond to such personal attention.

Q: What do I say to a parent who feels that her child's desire to read is affected by the labels and restrictions of the school's reading program?

A: Offer to work with the child to help her find books that interest her. The school may insist that the child participate in a computerized or controlled reading program, but the child may be quite willing to read beyond the reading requirements placed on her by the teacher. Suggest to the child and the parent that the child set her own reading goals. Maybe she is required to take a test on only one book a week. Ask the child to get that requirement out of the way and read other books because she wants to read them, not because she has to read them.

Q: What else can I do to help children who suffer through reading because of grade-level labeling and the requirement to win points for the class?

A: Make personalized reading lists for students who are struggling to find just the right reading material. Do not assume it is only poor readers who need your guidance. Ask the administration and faculty to drop the idea of winning points and prizes for reading. There are many ways to celebrate books and reading without assigning a point value to books based on number of pages or vocabulary level. Be persistent: it may take a while to convince them that this practice places labels on students and may actually stunt their growth as readers.

Q: What if reading is hard for a child? Children know when they are poor readers.

A: Yes, children do know when they are deficient readers, but they do not want this fact pointed out to their peers. Children should feel that a library media center is neutral territory, a place where they are equal to their peers. Guide such children to themed short story collections. Nonfiction also works well with reluctant readers. Connect a book to a movie or a television program.

Q: How can I find sufficient time to spend with children with special needs?

A: All children are special, and they all need our guidance if they are to achieve to the very best of their ability. Some children may demand more attention than others, but no child should be victim to a label or deserve any type of rejection in the school library media program. They must feel that the school library media center belongs to them, that they are free to use the services without bias or any type of prejudice.

Labels and Rating Systems: An Interpretation of the Library Bill of Rights

Libraries do not advocate the ideas found in their collections or in resources accessible through the library. The presence of books and other resources in a library does not indicate endorsement of their contents by the library. Likewise, the ability for library users to access electronic information using library computers does not indicate endorsement or approval of that information by the library.

Labels

Labels on library materials may be viewpoint-neutral directional aids that save the time of users, or they may be attempts to prejudice or discourage users or restrict their access to materials. When labeling is an attempt to prejudice attitudes, it is a censor's tool. The American Library Association opposes labeling as a means of predisposing people's attitudes toward library materials.

Prejudicial labels are designed to restrict access, based on a value judgment that the content, language or themes of the material, or the background or views of the creator(s) of the material, render it inappropriate or offensive for all or certain groups of users. The prejudicial label is used to warn, discourage or prohibit users or certain groups of users from accessing the material. Such labels may be used to remove materials from open shelves to restricted locations where access depends on staff intervention.

Viewpoint-neutral directional aids facilitate access by making it easier for users to locate materials. The materials are housed on open shelves and are equally accessible to all users, who may choose to consult or ignore the directional aids at their own discretion.

Directional aids can have the effect of prejudicial labels when their implementation becomes proscriptive rather than descriptive. When directional aids are used to forbid access or to suggest moral or doctrinal endorsement, the effect is the same as prejudicial labeling.

Rating Systems

A variety of organizations promulgate rating systems as a means of advising either their members or the general public concerning their opinions of the contents and suitability or appropriate age for use of certain books, films, recordings, Web sites, or other materials. The adoption, enforcement, or endorsement of any of these rating systems by the library violates the Library Bill of Rights. Adopting such systems into law may be unconstitutional. If such legislation is passed, the library should seek legal advice regarding the law's applicability to library operations.

Publishers, industry groups, and distributors sometimes add ratings to material or include them as part of their packaging. Librarians should not endorse such practices. However, removing or destroying such ratings—if placed there by, or with permission of, the copyright holder—could constitute expurgation (see Expurgation of Library Materials: An Interpretation of the Library Bill of Rights).

Some find it easy and even proper, according to their ethics, to establish criteria for judging materials as objectionable. However, injustice and ignorance, rather than justice and enlightenment, result from such practices. The American Library Association opposes any efforts that result in closing any path to knowledge.

Adopted July 13, 1951, by the ALA Council; amended June 25, 1971; July 1, 1981; June 26, 1990; January 19, 2005.

level. Is it possible that Quint's mother is planning to read the book aloud to Quint? Should a school not promote such parent/child interaction?

These scenarios may help Mrs. Brown and others like her see how devastating labels are to students. Mrs. Brown is probably under pressure for her students to achieve well on the state-mandated tests. But the library media center should have programs and practices to help Mrs. Brown turn her students into readers. This will not happen if students are held prisoner to the labels assigned to them. ■

CASE STUDY 2
Student Privacy and Time Management

Kevin is in the library media center with his economics class. Their assignment is to follow the price of ten different stocks for the previous two weeks. The library media specialist notices that Kevin is playing a game rather than working on the assignment.

Kevin has a specific assignment, and the library media specialist should view herself as a part of the teaching team. It is easy to tell when a student is not managing his time well without breaching his privacy. Rather than report Kevin to his teacher, it is appropriate to approach Kevin and point him to the website where he can find the stock quotes. In this way, he is not reprimanded but directed. Tell Kevin that he may save the site he is on, or record the URL, so that he can return to it once his assignment is complete. It is not necessary to even note the site Kevin is using. ■

Privacy for Families

Mrs. Wood calls a middle school media specialist and asks if he can help her identify books that deal with death. She tells the media specialist that her father has just died and that her sixth-grade son is having a tough time dealing with his grandfather's death. She does not want the media specialist to tell her son that she called.

Mrs. Wood obviously feels that the media specialist is the person who can best help her. This is a good opportunity for the library to serve a parent as well as the child. There must be a reason that Mrs. Wood does not want her son to know that she made the telephone call. Maybe she feels that her son's grief is too personal, that he would not want to express any emotion at school. Her reason does not matter; it is good that she wants to use books to help her son during this tough time.

The media specialist should make an annotated list of books that he feels may appeal to the needs of the student and mail the list to Mrs. Wood. In this way, Mrs. Wood and her son can sit down and talk about the books that they might read together. The media specialist should take care to keep Mrs. Wood's call confidential, even from such school personnel as the guidance counselor. Let Mrs. Wood call the guidance counselor if she decides that she needs her services. ■

Library Records

Mary is in the eighth grade, and she needs to use library resources to complete a science project. She approaches the circulation desk with a stack of books, but the media specialist says to her, "Mary, you checked out five books on drugs last year and did not return a single one. You have to pay your debts."

There are several layers to this problem: labeling, privacy, and access. First, this type of comment labels Mary as a person who loses books. Second, it infringes on her privacy by revealing that she checked out books on drugs. Third, the library media specialist is denying Mary access to the materials she needs. It is possible that Mary has grown into a more responsible person and should not bear the label of being "irresponsible" for the remainder of her school years. Her family's financial status may prohibit her from paying for the lost materials.

Mary and her library transactions may be protected under state privacy law. If she is not, the library media specialist needs to consider a more ethical response. It is okay to remind Mary that she still has not paid for her lost materials, but this reminder should be done in complete privacy. Even then, the conversation should let Mary know that she is welcome in the library media center and that she is allowed materials. The type of materials that Mary lost is not the issue and should not be discussed with her. Mary should be the only person who knows what materials she checked out. ■

Law Enforcement and Requests for Library Records

From time to time, law enforcement officers may come to the library media center and ask the library media specialist to turn over a student's library records. In most circumstances, however, the law does not permit either federal agents or police officers to demand a student's library records or confidential information without first providing some form of *judicial process*—a subpoena, a search warrant, or other legally enforceable order—to the school holding the library records.

A *subpoena* is the most common means used to compel an institution to hand over library records. A subpoena is issued by a grand jury or court and is usually signed by the prosecuting attorney; sometimes the subpoena is signed by a judge. The subpoena identifies the records that are sought for the investigation and instructs the library media specialist to provide those records at a certain date, time, and place.

The library media specialist should carefully examine the subpoena with the school's legal counsel to assure that it was issued correctly and contains all required signatures, information, and notices. If the library media specialist or school's legal counsel believes that the subpoena is unjustified for any reason, the school's legal counsel can file a motion to quash the subpoena before a court with jurisdiction over the investigation.

A *search warrant* is a court order that authorizes law enforcement officers to search for and seize particular items in a particular location. It is issued by a court and signed by a judge after a hearing to determine if "probable cause" exists—that is, whether there is good cause to believe the search will produce evidence of a crime. The police officer may serve the search warrant on the school at any time, and the library media specialist will be required to permit the search for the records or items listed in the search warrant or to provide the officer with those records or items.

Since a search warrant authorizes the police to conduct the search without notice and without delay, there is little or no opportunity to challenge a search warrant in a court of law before the school is required to comply. Even so, the library media specialist should inform the administration and the school's legal counsel as soon as possible.

FISA orders are court orders authorized by the Foreign Intelligence Surveillance Act (FISA), as amended by Section 215 of the USA PATRIOT Act. FISA orders are issued by the Foreign Intelligence Surveillance Court and authorize FBI agents to seize "any tangible thing," including documents, records, computer disks, and any other physical object, as long as the FBI agent alleges that the item is relevant to an ongoing investigation into terrorism or foreign espionage. Under Section 215, a party served with a FISA order is subject to an automatic non-disclosure order, or "gag order," that forbids recipients of a FISA order from disclosing to anyone that they have received a FISA order or that records have been turned over to the FBI. The PATRIOT Act allows the recipient of a FISA order to challenge the order in the FISA court, but the court will not quash a FISA order unless the court finds it "unlawful." The gag order may be challenged in the FISA court one year after the service of the FISA order.

National Security Letters (NSL) are specialized, written orders to turn over records that are issued by the FBI. Section 505 of the USA PATRIOT Act expanded the FBI's authority to utilize these orders to obtain certain types of records, including electronic communication records that may be held by a library providing Internet services. Like recipients of FISA orders, NSL recipients are subject to a nondisclosure order forbidding any recipient from disclosing the existence of the NSL or that records were turned over to the FBI.

The law authorizes the FBI to issue these orders without any judicial review or supervision by a court. Refusal to comply with the order or violation of the nondisclosure order is a crime. A recipient of an NSL can, however, challenge the legality of an NSL and its accompanying gag order in a federal district court.

All schools and library media centers, public or private, should have written policies and procedures for handling subpoenas, search warrants, and PATRIOT Act orders. Such written policies assure that every request for records is handled in accordance with the law. It is important to remember that, even if a state's library confidentiality statute does not require law enforcement officers to obtain a court order to examine school library records, the Family Educational Rights and Privacy Act (FERPA) forbids the disclosure of a student's records unless the parent provides written consent or the officer presents the school with a court order.

Sample policies for handling law enforcement requests can be found on the ALA website (see below).

Additional Resources

Family Educational Rights and Privacy Act, 20 U.S.C. 1232g

Gotham City Model Policy 1.1: www.ala.org/ala/aboutala/offices/oif/ifissues/issuesrelatedlinks/model_lawenforcement_policy4.doc

Gotham City Model Staff Directive 1.5: www.ala.org/ala/aboutala/offices/oif/ifissues/issuesrelatedlinks/model_lawenforcement_procedure4.doc

State Privacy Laws regarding Library Records: www.ala.org/ala/aboutala/offices/oif/ifgroups/stateifcchairs/stateifcinaction/stateprivacy.cfm

Library Records and the Law

A student is accused of a rape in the neighborhood where he lives. Local law enforcement does not have enough evidence on the student to make an arrest. They come to the school in an effort to gather information about the student's reading habits, websites he has visited, and the like. The principal brings the law officer to the library media center and asks that the media specialist access the student's library records.

The library media specialist should not turn over the student's library records unless the law officer has a subpoena. The school administrator and the police officer should be reminded of the confidentiality of library records law. It is recommended that library media records be "dumped" once students have returned materials. In this way, the library media specialist is not placed in a difficult situation with the school administration and the local police. Unless the law officer has more than circumstantial evidence, it is not likely that he will go so far as to take computer hard drives. It would be difficult to prove what Internet sites any student has visited unless the library media center requires student log-ins on all computers in the media center. Such log-ins should be avoided in an effort to protect student privacy. ■

ALA Position Statement on the Confidentiality of Library Records

The members of the American Library Association [ALA Policy 52.4 (see below), 54.16], recognizing the right to privacy of library users, believe that records held in libraries which connect specific individuals with specific resources, programs or services, are confidential and not to be used for purposes other than routine record keeping: i.e., to maintain access to resources, to assure that resources are available to users who need them, to arrange facilities, to provide resources for the comfort and safety of patrons, or to accomplish the purposes of the program or service. The library community recognizes that children and youth have the same rights to privacy as adults.

Libraries whose record keeping systems reveal the names of users would be in violation of the confidentiality of library record laws adopted in many states. School library media specialists are advised to seek the advice of counsel if in doubt about whether their record keeping systems violate the specific laws in their states. Efforts must be made within the reasonable constraints of budgets and school management procedures to eliminate such records as soon as reasonably possible.

With or without specific legislation, school library media specialists are urged to respect the rights of children and youth by adhering to the tenets expressed in the Confidentiality of Library Records Interpretation of the Library Bill of Rights and the ALA Code of Ethics.

ALA Policy 52.4 Confidentiality of Library Records

The ethical responsibilities of librarians, as well as statues in most states and the District of Columbia, protect the privacy of library users. Confidentiality extends to "information sought or received, and materials consulted, borrowed, acquired," and includes database search records, interlibrary loan records, and other personally identifiable uses of library materials, facilities, or services.

The American Library Association recognizes that law enforcement agencies and officers may occasionally believe that library records contain information which may be helpful to the investigation of criminal activity. If there is a reasonable basis to believe such records are necessary to the progress of an investigation or prosecution, the American judicial system provides mechanism for seeking release of such confidential records: the issuance of a court order, following a showing of good cause based on specific facts, by a court of competent jurisdiction.

The American Library Association strongly recommends that the responsible officers in each library, cooperative system, and consortium in the United States:

1. Formally adopt a policy which specifically recognizes its circulation records and other records identifying the names of library users with specific materials to be confidential.
2. Advise all librarians and library employees that such records shall not be made available to any agency of state, federal, or local government except pursuant to such process, order, or subpoena as may be authorized under the authority of, and pursuant to, federal, state, or local law relating to civil, criminal, or administrative discovery procedures or legislative investigatory power.
3. Resist the issuance or enforcement of such process, order, or subpoena until such time as a proper showing of good cause has been made in a court of competent jurisdiction.

(Revised July 1999)

Sample Library Confidentiality Statute

22 V.S.A. § 171 (2008)
Library Patron Records

§ 171 Definitions
As used in this chapter,

(1) "library" means a public library as defined in subdivision 101(2) of this title, any college university or school library, or any other library or archives that are open on a regular basis and makes available on site, or circulates, materials to the public without a fee.

(2) "patron registration records" means library records that contain information a library patron must provide in order to be eligible for borrowing privileges at a library.

(3) "patron transaction records" means library records that contain names or other personal identifying information that discloses an individual's activities within a library, including the materials that have been viewed in print or electronic form, research questions posed, materials in any format that the patron has requested through interlibrary loan or has borrowed, or any other library service or consultation that the patron has requested.

§ 172 Library record confidentiality; exemptions

(A) a library's patron registration records and patron transaction records shall remain confidential.

(B) unless authorized by other provisions of law, the library's officers, employees, and volunteers shall not disclose the records except:

(1) with the written permission of the library patron to whom the records pertain;

(2) to officers, employees, volunteers, and agents of the library to the extent necessary for library administration purposes;

(3) in response to an authorized judicial order or warrant directing disclosure;

(4) to custodial parents or guardians of patrons under age 16;

(5) to the custodial parents or guardians of a student, in accordance with the federal family educational rights and privacy act, by the library at the school the student attends.

(C) statistical records pertaining to the patronage, circulation activities, and use of any service or consultation the library provides, provided that they do not contain the names of patrons or any other personally identifying information, shall be exempt from the provisions of this chapter.

§ 173 Right of Patron Action

Any person whose confidential patron registration records or patron transaction records have been disclosed, except as provided in this chapter, is authorized to bring a civil action against the library that disclosed the records.

Additional Resource

State Privacy Laws regarding Library Records: www.ala.org/ala/aboutala/offices/oif/ifgroups/stateifcchairs/stateifcinaction/stateprivacy.cfm

Student E-mail

An eighth-grade girl is marked absent at school, and as a matter of routine the attendance clerk calls the girl's parents to check on her. The parents are surprised that their daughter is not in school, because they dropped her off at the school bus stop in their neighborhood that morning on their way to work. Other students at the bus stop reported that they saw her get in the car with a guy who looked to be in high school. When the girl does not come home that night, the parents call local law enforcement and report her missing. Since all students in the middle school are given e-mail accounts, the parents request that the IT department grant them access to their daughter's account.

In most circumstances, accessing a student's e-mail account by anyone other than the student is considered a violation of the student's confidentiality. In this case, however, the student may be in harm's way, and if her e-mail gives any clues to conversations with older guys she may be afforded a safe return. Students should receive safety tips for e-mailing, and they must understand that in the event of a serious issue regarding their safety the school will likely access their e-mail account. Students who are concerned about confidentiality should use their school account only for communication with teachers and peers regarding schoolwork and functions and have a private account for all other communication. ■

Overdue Notices

Overdue notices are sent to students in homeroom at the end of each week. The notices are stapled with the student name written on the outside of the notice. Teachers are asked to give the notices to the students. Jack, a tenth-grader, comes into the media center and brings a notice that bears the name of a classmate, Amy. He says that he has been waiting for this video and asks if the library staff can please tell Amy that she has to return it. The library media specialist explains to Jack that he should not know what Amy has checked out, and neither should he know that the video is overdue. Jack explains that he found the notice on the floor in the hallway.

The media specialist is correct to explain to Jack that Amy's library transactions should be kept private. However, the library staff made every effort to secure the notice and even requested that the teacher recognize the importance of this confidential information. If Amy is careless and drops her notice in the hallway or throws it away, and another student finds it, then the library media staff is not responsible. Students should be told during library media center orientation at the beginning of the school year about the importance of keeping their library records private. They must understand that the library media center is committed to student privacy, but they must be responsible for their own privacy as well.

Explain to Jack that the material will be placed on hold for him and that he will be notified when the material has been returned. He should be instructed to destroy the notice and not to approach Amy with this information. ■

Labeling and Privacy Checklist

- ☐ What are the state privacy laws?
- ☐ Are the privacy laws posted in the library media center?
- ☐ What is the library media center's philosophy about reading-level labels?
- ☐ Do all library media center staff and volunteers understand the proper response to a law enforcement request to access a student's library records?
- ☐ Do the administration and faculty understand the connection between reading-level labels and a child's right to privacy?
- ☐ Do the faculty understand the library media specialist's role in dealing with time management issues?
- ☐ How do the state's privacy laws apply to overdue library notices?

CHAPTER 5

Internet Access

The Internet reaffirms what we instinctively know. Words aren't powerful.
Indeed, information isn't powerful. Only knowledge is powerful.

Arthur Sulzberger Jr., publisher

The primary purpose of a school media program is to help students achieve knowledge. It seems somewhat paradoxical, then, that the one place where students should be free to obtain and try out knowledge is the place where they are most likely blocked from a vast amount of information—the World Wide Web. Students are expected to graduate with a basic knowledge of many different subjects, yet that knowledge is controlled. They are asked to be responsible users of information, yet the information they are allowed is often filtered, and therefore limited.

> **The (Internet) block list is what we all hate. It is the bane of every student and teacher. . . . If you don't understand it, ban it.**
>
> *Daniel Silverman, student, 2001*

It is difficult for schools to help students take that final leap toward knowledge when state and federal government regulations bar open access to the Web.

Though a few schools manage to offer unfiltered Internet access to students, schools that accept the federal discounted e-rate for Internet access are required to put filters on their network or on individual computers. Some states require all schools to filter the Internet or lose state funding. These types of laws leave schools that depend on state and federal funding with no option but to filter. Even in schools where filtering software is not mandatory, some school personnel, including library media specialists, like the idea of limiting students' access to the Internet because they feel that filtering relieves them of any personal liability should a student access an "inappropriate" site. Companies that design filtering software actually promote this belief.

But school personnel and parents must know that there is no filter that is fool-proof. Students who are technologically savvy may find a way around filters, and other students may accidentally access a site that somehow dodged the filter. At the same time, it is important to note that filters do often block constitutionally protected speech. School personnel must understand these issues in order to do the best job possible of preparing students to be responsible users of the Internet within the constraints of federal and state laws.

The Internet has become a "culture" among students, and access to the vast amount of material that it offers is expected in a school library media center. All school personnel must understand that information on the Internet should, for the most part, be considered a vital resource for student research needs.

Because the Internet has become a home reference tool for many students and is likely the only source of information for most families, it is necessary for teachers and school library media specialists to deal with the challenges that this technology poses in the learning environment. Plagiarism and copyright issues come up with every term paper assignment; misinformation clouds students' minds and interferes with their ability to make informed decisions about the validity of information found on the Internet; and blogs, wikis, and social networking sites such as Facebook contribute to occasional disciplinary matters in schools. Although most students know how to navigate the Internet, most do not have the skills to distinguish opinion from fact, or truth from fiction. This is a skill that needs to be taught, beginning in the early elementary grades. It is not enough to know how to access information. Students must become discerning learners if they are to function successfully in the technological world in which they live. Only then can students begin the long journey toward knowledge.

CASE STUDY 1

Internet Use Policy

The principal of a high school thinks that the school should have some statement about student use of the Internet in the student handbook. Since the school district filters the network, students have little chance of accessing sites that may be deemed inappropriate by school personnel or parents. The student handbook committee considers putting such a policy in the student handbook unnecessary.

Every school needs an Internet acceptable-use policy, and the policy needs to be issued to every parent and student. Not only should the policy be included in the student

Reasons for a School Internet Acceptable-Use Policy

- To let parents know the school's expectations regarding Internet use.
- To inform students about privileges and responsibilities regarding Internet use.
- To educate students about the vast amount of information available on the Internet and the steps they should take toward identifying legitimate sites.
- To explain proper Internet etiquette, including respect for others and their private property.
- To warn students against disclosing personal identification on the Internet.
- To outline how rules of behavior are enforced.
- To give details about legal issues, such as copyright infringement and plagiarism.
- To discourage any type of illegal behavior, such as personal harassment.
- To set rules for e-mail use, in the event the school issues e-mail accounts to students.
- To establish rules regarding social networking sites.

Federal Laws Regulating Internet Access

Children's Internet Protection Act, 47 U.S.C. § 254(h)(5) and 20 U.S.C. § 9134(f)

The Children's Internet Protection Act (CIPA) requires public schools and libraries that wish to receive federal e-rate discounts or Library Services and Technology Act (LSTA) grant payments for Internet access to certify that they have adopted an Internet use policy that includes a "technology protection measure," that is, blocking or filtering technology.

The filtering technology must be installed on all computers in the school, including computers used by faculty and staff. It must be configured to block minors' access to visual depictions that are obscene, child pornography, or harmful to minors; it must also block adults' access to visual depictions that are obscene or child pornography.

CIPA permits an administrator to disable the technology during use by an adult in order to permit access for "bona fide research or other lawful purposes." The law does not forbid unblocking a wrongfully

blocked website that does not contain materials that meet the law's criteria for blocking.

CIPA imposes no requirements on schools and libraries that do not receive federal e-rate discounts or LSTA grants.

Neighborhood Children's Internet Protection Act (47 U.S.C. § 254[l])

The Neighborhood Children's Internet Protection Act (NCIPA) requires public schools and libraries receiving federal e-rate discounts to draft and implement an Internet safety policy. The policy must address the following issues:

- Access by minors to inappropriate matter on the Internet and World Wide Web.
- The safety and security of minors when using electronic mail, chat rooms, and other forms of direct electronic communications.
- Unauthorized access, including so-called hacking, and other unlawful activities by minors online.

- Unauthorized disclosure, use, and dissemination of personal identification information regarding minors.
- Measures designed to restrict minors' access to materials harmful to minors.

Before adopting the Internet safety policy, the school or library must hold at least one public hearing or meeting to allow the community to address the proposed policy.

NCIPA states that the determination of material as "inappropriate" is left to the local school board, educational agency, or library; no federal agency may interfere in that determination. The determination of policy details to adopt is left solely to the discretion of the local body.

Children's Online Privacy Protection Act 15 U.S.C. § 6501

The Children's Online Privacy Protection Act (COPPA) requires commercial websites and online services that collect, use, or disclose personal information from children under age thirteen to take certain steps to protect the children's personal information.

The website owner must

- Provide notice on the website of what information is collected from children, how the website owner uses such information, and the owner's disclosure practices for such information.
- Obtain verifiable parental consent for the collection, use, or disclosure of personal information from children.

COPPA does not impose any duties on schools, library media centers, or library media specialists, but it can affect how students thirteen and younger use online services in the classroom and library media center.

Other Laws Regulating Internet Access

At the present time, twenty-one states have Internet filtering laws that apply to public schools or libraries. Most of these laws require only that schools or libraries adopt Internet use policies that address minors' access to online materials that are obscene, "harmful to minors," or are child pornography. A small number of states require public schools or libraries to install filtering software on computers. The National Conference of State Legislatures maintains a frequently updated website (link below) with information about state laws regulating Internet use or access.

Additional Resources

Bocher, Robert, *FAQ on E-rate Compliance with the Children's Internet Protection Act:* http://dpi.wi.gov/pld/pdf/cipafaq.pdf

Federal Communications Commission, *In the Matter of Federal-State Joint Board on Universal Service Children's Internet Protection Act, CC Docket No. 96-45 (July 24, 2003):* http://hraunfoss.fcc.gov/edocs_public/attachmatch/FCC-03-188A1.pdf

Institute of Museum and Library Services, *The Children's Internet Protection Act:* www.imls.gov/about/cipa.shtm

National Conference of State Legislatures, *State Internet Filtering Laws:* www.ncsl.org/programs/lis/CIP/filterlaws.htm

United States Federal Trade Commission, *Frequently Asked Questions about the Children's Online Privacy Protection Rule:* www.ftc.gov/privacy/coppafaqs.shtm

handbook, it should also be posted on the school's website. Some schools even ask students and parents to sign an acceptable-use agreement so that it can be filed and reviewed with students in the event that "unacceptable" Internet behavior occurs. Schools should let students and parents know that many filters have proven ineffective, and that it is quite possible that information considered inappropriate may actually bypass the filter.

Parents and students should know the school's philosophy and expectations regarding Internet use. In addition to an acceptable-use policy, schools may wish to conduct parent/student workshops. Students might help their parents navigate the Internet in the school's library media center or in the classrooms. Make sure that all parties understand that what is "inappropriate" or "objectionable" to one user may not be to another. Explain to students and their parents that the same rules of individual privacy regarding use of library materials apply to Internet use. Students and parents also need to know the school or school district's policy about unblocking filtered sites when students make the request. How and to whom should such a request be made? What is the time frame for unblocking a site? How will students be notified that the unblocked site is available?

Acceptable-use policies should be evaluated each year to accommodate new issues that may have come up during the school year. The rules outlined in the policy should be reasonable, and the language not too strident. Students must have access to the Internet to function in a school environment today. To limit their use, or to make the rules of behavior too harsh, is in effect to impede access to information and knowledge. ■

Components of an Internet Acceptable-Use Policy

Statement of Policy

Example: Internet access is provided to students in all of the schools in the district. The Internet offers vast and unique resources to teachers and students. All users are expected to follow guidelines established by the school and school district.

Access Rights and Privileges

Statement of school district's right to place responsibility and restriction on users.

Statement regarding e-mail accounts, either on school network or external e-mail accounts.

Failure to abide by the guidelines outlined in this policy could result in a suspension of privileges.

Statement of students' right to request that specific site be unblocked for research purposes.

Unacceptable Use

Illegal activity, such as violation of copyright.

Downloading software without authorization.

Gaining unauthorized access to resources or entities.

Using the network for commercial or private advertising.

Accessing and displaying patently offensive sites.

Revealing personal identity (name, personal address, telephone number, social security number) except in cases such as a common college application.

Network Etiquette

Be polite.

Use appropriate language (no swear words or vulgarities).

Respect privacy of others.

Close out all windows when computer sessions are complete.

Security

If a security problem can be identified, notify a teacher or administrator.

Do not demonstrate the security problem to other users.

Do not use another person's account without written permission from that person.

A statement of disciplinary action regarding attempts to log on to the system as an administrator or to compromise the security of the network.

Vandalism

A statement of disciplinary action regarding any malicious attempt to harm or destroy data on the schools network, which includes uploading of viruses.

Viruses

A statement releasing the school from any responsibility due to viruses that may or may not have been acquired on school computers.

Filters

A statement regarding compliance with the Children's Internet Protection Act.

I worry about my child and the Internet all the time, even though she's too young to have logged on yet. Here's what I worry about. I worry that ten or fifteen years from now, she will come to me and say, "Daddy, where were you when they took freedom of the press away from the Internet?"

Mike Codwin

Students' Rights of Access

In compliance with federal funding laws, the school board filters students' Internet access at all levels. As part of its policymaking, the board adopted a generalized policy permitting unblocking for legitimate research purposes. At the beginning of the semester, all students taking AP Biology are assigned a comprehensive research project on such subjects as abortion, sexuality, genetic manipulation, and the correlation between substance abuse and infertility. The project is due at the end of the term, but the filter is preventing students from accessing the information they need. Both the library media specialist and the AP Biology teacher ask that the filter be disabled for the students' research. The director of the IT department refuses, claiming that most of the sites fail to meet "harmful to minors" standards set by the federal funding law.

This is a common problem in schools where the IT department operates independently of the school library. In this case, the school board has a written policy that allows students to request that specific sites be unblocked for educational purposes. It is not the role of the IT department to make judgments about the content of the sites students need. Remind the IT department that the "harmful to minors" clause in the Children's Internet Protection Act clearly states that any material that is "literary, artistic, political, or has scientific value to minors" is allowed. Therefore, the Internet information needed for the AP Biology class project is allowable.

In an ideal situation, the school library media specialist, teacher, and IT department would meet and discuss the assignment, the sites the students are likely to need, and the time frame for making the sites available.

Since this is a long-term project, there is time for students to meet with the library media specialist and make a plan for conducting research. At this time, the library media specialist should offer instruction in using the Internet as a reference tool. This training should include how to evaluate content on the Internet, identify reliable information, and properly cite Web resources. Students should also know the proper procedure for requesting that a site be unblocked. Since a minor is defined as anyone under age seventeen, it is likely that the majority of the students in the AP Biology class are minors. Students should be aware of the law, and they should understand that, although they have a right to the information they need to complete an assignment, they must also be responsible users of the Internet. For example, if a website includes images that someone may deem inappropriate, such as an actual or simulated sexual act, the students should take the information they need and exit the site immediately. Such responsible use creates an element of trust that ultimately affects the entire student population and their right to have access to the Internet and all that it offers.

Many school library catalogs allow the capability to drop a website URL into the catalog. In this way, websites that have been researched by students, and found to be helpful, may be included in the catalog so that they are easily available by subject or keyword search. The problem is that a site on a subject like "abortion" may be unblocked by the IT department for a one-time use by a student. The irony is that the library media center may actually have many print materials that deal with the subject. This may actually contribute to the argument to permanently unblock a site. ■

"Harmful to Minors" Laws and the Library Media Center

In *Ginsberg v. New York,* the Supreme Court ruled that federal and state legislators may regulate or restrict minors' access to sexually explicit speech protected by the Constitution. In upholding New York's law forbidding the sale of sexually explicit material to minors, the court reasoned that minors' First Amendment rights are more limited than adults' First Amendment rights, and that the government has a compelling interest in aiding parents' efforts to shield children from certain categories of indecent, sexually explicit speech. But the court warned that any such restrictions must be narrowly tailored so that adults' access to constitutionally protected, sexually explicit speech is not impaired.

As a result, Congress and state legislatures have passed laws restricting or regulating the dissemination of sexually explicit materials to minors. Under the standards set by *Ginsberg,* such laws, called "harmful to minors" or "obscene-as-to-minors" laws, must include safeguards for speech that is protected by the Constitution. Thus, such laws must protect minors' access to sexually themed speech that has serious literary, artistic, scientific, or political value for minors and may not restrict adults' rights to access nonobscene speech.

For example, the Children's Internet Protection Act (CIPA) narrowly defines the categories of speech that are deemed to be "harmful to minors" for the purposes of filtering Internet content:

> *Harmful to minors.* The term "harmful to minors" means any picture, image, graphic image file, or other visual depiction that
> (i) taken as a whole and with respect to minors, appeals to a prurient interest in nudity, sex, or excretion;
> (ii) depicts, describes, or represents, in a patently offensive way with respect to what is suitable for minors, an actual or simulated sexual act or sexual contact, actual or simulated normal or perverted sexual acts, or a lewd exhibition of the genitals; and
> (iii) taken as a whole, lacks serious literary, artistic, political, or scientific value as to minors. (47 U.S.C. 254[h][7][G])

CIPA defines a minor as "any individual who has not attained the age of 17 years" (47 U.S.C. 254[h][7][D]).

To be found "harmful to minors" by a court of law, the material must meet all three requirements outlined in the law and must be measured against what is "harmful to minors" for the oldest minor rather than the youngest minor. In addition, "harmful to minors" statutes may not be applied so as to block access to all materials containing nudity or addressing sexual matters when only a small number of those items could be deemed obscene for minors.

Library media specialists should know and understand state and federal laws restricting access to obscenity, child pornography, and "harmful to minors" materials. Many obscenity and "harmful to minors" laws apply only to commercial transactions involving the sale or rental of these materials. Other states, recognizing the educational mission of schools and libraries, provide exemptions for schools and libraries that may collect and provide materials for education and research that some persons may deem indecent.

Additional Resources

Ginsberg v. New York, 390 U.S. 629 (1968)

Miller v. California, 413 U.S. 15 (1973)

Reno v. ACLU, 524 U.S. 844 (1997)

Sable Communications of California, Inc. v. FCC, 492 U.S. 115 (1989)

Student Responsibility

George is in the seventh grade and is a whiz on the computer and the Internet. He has hacked through the school's filter and is visiting Japanese manga websites, including sites with sexually explicit images. After he takes home printouts of some of these images, his parents call the school board to claim that the school library media specialist should have supervised George's use of the Internet and made sure that he did not access sites that his parents do not approve of.

First, the school board should have a statement in its Internet use policy that makes it perfectly clear to parents and students that filters do not always work. The responsibility for appropriate use of the school's computer terminals and access to the Internet should be placed on the student. This is one of the arguments for requiring student and parent signatures on the Internet use policy. Second, the very nature of the services rendered in a school library media center relieves the school library media specialist of any legal responsibility in a case like George's. The library media specialist is often the only adult in the library media center. He cannot, and should not, be responsible for the activities of each student in the media center. George is a computer whiz and clearly understands what he has done, and it should be made clear to him and his parents that it is George alone who is the responsible party.

Furthermore, parents and students must understand that information on the Internet is used in a school library media setting in the same way print materials are used. The difference is that the print materials are selected as age appropriate for the majority of the students in the school. The nature of the Internet makes all kinds

Responsibility for Minors' Internet Use—*Kathleen R. v. City of Livermore*

The library has computers linked to the Internet, which patrons of any age are free to use. Twelve-year-old Brandon went to the computers without [his mother's] knowledge and downloaded sexually explicit photos from the Internet onto a floppy disk that he brought to the library. [Brandon's mother] alleges that the photos Brandon obtained are harmful to minors and that some of them are obscene.

When Brandon's mother, Kathleen R., learned about Brandon's activities, she filed a lawsuit against the City of Livermore and its public library. She claimed the library should be legally liable for providing obscene pornography to her minor son, even though the library did not itself exhibit the materials or teach Brandon how to access them.

A California appellate court ordered her lawsuit dismissed. It identified two reasons for rejecting her claims:

- The court held that Section 230 of the Telecommunications Act of 1996 provides libraries with immunity from lawsuits that seek to hold libraries liable for content provided by a third party and accessed through the Internet. The library was therefore entitled to immunity from Kathleen R.'s lawsuit. The court explained, "There is a crucial distinction between providing minors with harmful matter on the one hand, and maintaining computers where minors may obtain such matter, however easily, on the other."

- Kathleen R. could not claim that the library had a policy of providing obscene pornography to minors simply because it permitted minors to access the Internet without supervision. According to the court, "any such implication would be contrary to the library policy attached to the complaint, which among other things prohibits the use of computer resources for illegal purposes." It further noted that the library's policy warned users that controversial material is available on the Internet, that users who use Internet do so at their own risk, and that the library does not supervise minors' use of the Internet.

The result in *Kathleen R. v. City of Livermore* emphasizes the importance of having a comprehensive Internet use policy for the library media center. Such policies should inform parents and students about the guidelines for using computers, explain the consequences if those procedures are not followed, and state that the student and the student's parents are jointly responsible for the student's computer use. In addition, the policy should alert parents about the possibility of encountering controversial materials on the Internet and inform all users that computers are not to be used for illegal purposes, including accessing illegal materials on the Internet.

Additional Resources

Kathleen R. v. City of Livermore, 87 Cal. App. 4th 684 (2001)
Telecommunications Act of 1996, 47 U.S.C. §230

of information and images available that may not be age appropriate. For example, child pornography is illegal and therefore is not purchased for a school library. Child pornography is, however, available on the Internet. The school's filtering software attempts to block such sites, but there are always students like George who have the ability to hack through the filter.

Parents, students, and faculty should also understand that nudity is not considered pornography. A school will likely have an art book that includes an image of Michelangelo's *David*. Unfortunately, some sites on the Internet may actually filter an image of this statue, though students may find the statue on Google images or in Wikipedia. Accessing this image and other similar art materials is not improper behavior. ■

Student Websites

During the summer, a group of high school juniors developed a website through Yahoo so that they could stay in touch over the summer. The website requires a log-in. The students posted a picture of two classmates and captioned it "gay." A student logged in and printed the picture and gave it to the two boys pictured. The picture eventually landed into the hands of the assistant principal. He told the creators of the website that they would have to take it down.

The creators of the website may have made a poor choice to post the picture and caption, but the assistant principal cannot make the students take down the website. The website was created over the summer, it requires a log-in, and it was done through Yahoo and not on the school server or using school software. So it really is not a school issue. Although it is true that the website may have caused a ruckus among students at school, the assistant principal should use this time to help students understand proper etiquette and their responsibility toward one another. This is one of those prime teachable moments. Seize the opportunity. Chances are that the students will understand the ramifications of their actions, and I bet they will think before they post other statements that could cause hurt feelings.

Another way to explain this case to students is by comparing it to "slam books" that have existed in high schools for generations. These, too, are hurtful, and filled with malicious characterizations. But it is easier to control who is reading these books. Now, websites, even with log-ins, have a way of broadcasting comments to a large number of students at any given time. In the above case, some students made the unfortunate decision to print a picture and share it. These students should also accept some of the responsibility for causing the ruckus. ■

CASE STUDY 5

Student E-mail

All middle and high school students are issued e-mail accounts from the school. This is the way teachers communicate with them and one of the ways they can be in touch with class-

mates, especially in group assignments. Students do not want to use these e-mail accounts because they feel that the IT staff is reading their e-mail.

It is unethical for IT staff to read anyone's e-mail, but students must assume that their school e-mail account will not always be private. Advise them to use the school-issued e-mail account only for school use and to maintain a private e-mail account for personal use. Most students know about free e-mail accounts like Yahoo or Hotmail. Many students have paid e-mail accounts through their parents' network provider. Some schools do not allow students to use e-mail accounts, other than the school-issued accounts, on school computers. This is something that should be specified in the acceptable-use agreement, and students need to be reminded of this during library media center orientation. ■

CASE STUDY 6

Social Networking

Sarah is a senior in high school and has established a profile on MySpace. She has reported to the school counselor that she is being harassed by someone, and she thinks that it is a male student at another high school. Sarah posted her profile at home but does not want her parents to know. They disapprove of any type of Internet social networking. The counselor wants to call the other high school and have the counselor there talk with the student who Sarah thinks is the guilty party.

This is an issue that should be dealt with by Sarah and her parents. It appears that she has broken a rule at home, and it is not the school's responsibility to become involved in the investigation. The counselor should advise Sarah to tell her parents and help her understand where she went wrong with posting personal information. If Sarah is frightened and fears that the student from the other high school might show up at her school, then those who are on duty before and after school should be alerted to watch for outside visitors, especially if they are asking for Sarah.

Many schools do not allow students to participate in Internet social networking at school. Even so, it is appropriate for the school to conduct workshops with students and parents about the social networking culture. Students and parents need to understand that there is often no verification of membership on these sites, so it is quite possible for underage minors to participate. The primary reason for social networking is to share and discuss personal interests. Though most of these sites actually advise users against revealing personal information, many inexperienced and eager users find a way to release this information and are therefore vulnerable to harassment, threats, offensive e-mail, and the like. Many of these social networking sites have a "Classmate Finder," so they do encourage users to give the name and location of their school. It is appropriate for the school to share examples of personal profiles so that parents and students understand the entire culture of social networking. Some parents actually create a personal profile on MySpace and Facebook so that they can monitor the information their child is sharing.

If the school allows social networking, then clear guidelines for use should be communicated to students. These guidelines should stress the importance of safety on such sites. Ask students to become involved in setting such guidelines. They may think of safety tips that adults may not consider. ■

Internet Access Checklist

❏ Does the school district have a board policy regarding Internet use?

❏ Does the school ask students and parents to sign an acceptable-use policy?

❏ Does the Internet use policy include a procedure for unblocking sites to accommodate students' research needs?

❏ What is the role of the IT department?

❏ Do parents understand that students, and not the library media specialist, are responsible for student use of materials, including those from the Internet?

❏ Are the policies regarding social networking, student websites, and e-mail clear to students and their parents?

❏ Does the school support informal and formal workshops with students to help them grasp the enormity of their responsibility regarding Internet use?

Minors' First Amendment Rights to Access Information

Theresa Chmara

The U.S. Supreme Court long has recognized that minors enjoy some degree of First Amendment protection. It was well established in the landmark *Tinker* case that students do not "shed their constitutional rights to freedom of speech or expression at the schoolhouse gate." *Tinker v. Des Moines Indep. Community Sch. Dist.,* 393 U.S. 503, 506 (1969). In *Tinker,* the Supreme Court ordered a public school to allow students to wear black armbands in protest of the Vietnam War, explaining that "in our system, students may not be regarded as closed-circuit recipients of only that which the State chooses to communicate." *Id.* at 511. More recently, an appellate court considering the constitutionality of an ordinance restricting minors' access to certain video arcade games echoed the *Tinker* court's admonition that minors must have a broad range of information for intellectual growth, holding that "people are unlikely to become well-functioning, independent-minded adults and responsible citizens if they are raised in an intellectual bubble." *American Amusements Machine v. Kendrick,* 244 F.3d 572, 577 (7th Cir. 2001). Building on the recognition that access to information is fundamentally necessary, courts have held that minors' First Amendment liberties include the right to receive information and plainly extend beyond schools.

In *Board of Education v. Pico,* 457 U.S. 853 (1982) (plurality opinion), a school board had attempted to remove from a school library controversial titles such as *Slaughterhouse-Five* and *Soul on Ice.* The school board's action did not restrict minors' own expression, as the ban on armbands in *Tinker* had, but the Supreme Court rejected the action because the board was restricting what minors could read. The Court stated that "the right to receive ideas is a necessary predicate to the recipient's meaningful exercise of his own rights of speech, press, and political freedom," *id.* at 867, and made clear that "students too are beneficiaries of this principle." *Id.* at 868.[1]

The Supreme Court has limited minors' right to receive information in two instances in which adults' constitutional rights remain broader. First, the court has given public schools significant latitude to restrict minors' receipt of information if the school's judgment is based objectively on the fact that information is "educationally unsuitable" rather than on an official's subjective disagreement with or disapproval of the content of the information. The *Pico* plurality held unconstitutional the removal of books from school libraries where the removal was based on the ideas the books expressed but permitted removal of books if officials were motivated by concerns that the books were "educationally unsuitable" or "pervasively vulgar." *Pico,* 457 U.S. at 871. The plurality also recognized that schools must have substantial discretion in designing curricula. *Id.* at 864.

The second restriction on minors' right to receive information is that states may deem certain materials "obscene" for minors even if the materials are protected for adults. In *Ginsberg v. New York,* 390 U.S. 629 (1968), the Court upheld the conviction of a magazine vendor for selling an adult magazine to a sixteen-year-old. The Court explained that, although the magazine clearly was not "obscene" for adults, the state had acted within First Amendment bounds in adopting a distinct, broader definition of obscenity for minors. Because obscene speech enjoys no First Amendment protection, under *Ginsberg* states may completely bar minors from receiving material deemed obscene for them but not for adults. Accordingly, most states have enacted "harmful to minors" obscenity statutes. In *FCC v. Pacifica Foundation,* 438 U.S. 726 (1978), the Supreme Court restricted the broadcast of speech that was merely "indecent," not "obscene as to minors" under *Ginsberg,* largely because children might hear the indecent speech. See *id.* at 749–50. The Court, however, has declined to extend *Pacifica* to other media, including telephone communications, see *Sable Communications of California v. FCC,* 492 U.S. 115, 127–28 (1989), and, most notably, the Internet. See *Reno v. ACLU,* 524 U.S. 844, 864–65 (1997).

Moreover, courts have recognized limits on the *Ginsberg* principle. First, the Supreme Court has made clear that states may not simply ban minors' exposure to a full category of speech, such as nudity, when only a subset of that category can plausibly be deemed "obscene" for them. See *Erznoznik v. City of Jacksonville,* 422 U.S. 205, 212–14 (1975). Second, courts have held that states must determine *Ginsberg* "obscenity" by reference to the entire population of minors—including the oldest minors. One of the grounds on which the Supreme Court in *Reno* distinguished *Ginsberg* was that the "harmful to minors" statute at issue in *Ginsberg* did not apply to seventeen-year-olds, whereas the Communications Decency Act at issue in *Reno* did. See *Reno,* 524 U.S. at 864–65. The Court went on to stress "that the strength of the Government's interest in protecting minors is not equally strong throughout the [age] coverage of this broad statute." *Id.* at 878. Likewise, some lower courts have upheld restrictions on displays of adult magazines only if the restrictions did not prohibit the display of materials that would be appropriate for older minors. *American Booksellers v. Webb,* 919 F.2d 1493, 1504–05 (11th Cir. 1990); *American Booksellers Assn. v. Virginia,* 882 F.2d 125, 127 (4th Cir. 1989).

Minors in School and in the School Library

Although minors do not shed their First Amendment rights at the "schoolhouse gate," the Supreme Court has held that students' speech rights are not "automatically coextensive with the rights of adults in other settings," *Bethel School District No. 403 v. Fraser,* 478 U.S. 675, 682 (1986), and has generally applied those rights "in light of the special characteristics of the school environment." *Pico,* 457 U.S. at 868 (quoting *Tinker,* 393 U.S. at 506). In *Pico,* for example, although the Court's plurality opinion prohibited school officials from removing school library books based on the officials' disagreement with the ideas expressed in the books, it noted that removal decisions motivated by concerns that a book was "educationally unsuitable" or "pervasively vulgar" would be constitutional. *Id.* at 871.

Likewise, the Court in *Hazelwood School District v. Kuhlmeier,* 484 U.S. 267 (1988), permitted a high school principal to order the removal of certain articles from a school newspaper. The newspaper, which was written and edited by a student journalism class, had planned to run several controversial stories about student pregnancy and the impact of divorce on the school's students. The principal justified the removal decision on the grounds that the articles were inappropriate for the maturity level of the intended readers, the privacy interests of the articles' subjects were not adequately protected, and there was a danger that the controversial views would be attributed to the school. *Id.* at 274. The Supreme Court rejected the students' First Amendment claims, finding that a lower standard of review should apply when there is a danger that student expression will be perceived as "bear[ing] the imprimatur of the school." *Id.* at 271, 273 (holding that curriculum decisions are permissible if they are "reasonably related to legitimate pedagogical concerns").

Similarly, in *Bethel School District,* the Court held that a student could be disciplined for having delivered a speech that was "sexually explicit" (but not legally obscene) at an official school assembly. 478 U.S. at 685–86. In upholding the school's disciplinary action, the Court found it "perfectly appropriate for the school to disassociate itself to make the point to the pupils that vulgar speech and lewd conduct is wholly inconsistent with the 'fundamental values' of public school education." *Id.*

Hazelwood and *Bethel School District* are significant decisions but are of limited application to disputes involving student speech rights in public school libraries. School officials certainly cannot rely on those decisions to restrict students' speech at will, especially when that speech cannot reasonably be perceived as bearing the imprimatur of the school. Moreover, although courts plainly have given school officials a greater degree of control over decisions related to the school curriculum, see, e.g., *Pico,* 457 U.S. at 864, these decisions do not directly implicate school libraries, which provide students with both curricular and extracurricular materials. See *id.* at 860.

Numerous lower-court decisions have recognized the distinction in *Hazelwood* between curricular and noncurricular speech restrictions. In applying the *Hazelwood* case to other situations, lower courts have applied greater deference to school officials attempting to control curricular speech restrictions. See, e.g., *Virgil v. School Bd. of Columbia County,* 862 F.2d 1517, 1520 (11th Cir. 1989) ("In matters pertaining to the curriculum, educators have been accorded greater control over expression than they may enjoy in other spheres of activity.").[2] In *Virgil,* for example, the court of appeals affirmed a school board's decision to remove selected portions of *The Miller's Tale* and *Lysistrata* from a humanities course curriculum. In upholding the removal, the court emphasized that the disputed materials remained in the school library, *id.* at 1523 n. 8, which, unlike a course curriculum, was a "repository for 'voluntary inquiry.'" *Id.* at 1525 (quoting *Pico,* 457 U.S. at 869); but see *Pratt v. Independent Sch. Dist. No. 831,* 670 F.2d 771, 779 (8th Cir. 1982) (refusing to allow a school board to strike a short story, "The Lottery," from the school curriculum merely because the story remained available in the school library).

Students' First Amendment rights in the school library context, therefore, are broader than those in a class, school-sponsored assembly, or other curriculum-based activities. In the context of book removals from libraries, courts must make the determination whether the removal is based on educational suitability or is an attempt to impose viewpoint or content discrimination.

Minors in the Library

Recent decisions of lower federal courts have echoed the reasoning and the result of *Pico* and further clarified the rights of minors. For example, in *Campbell v. St. Tammany Parish School Board,* 64 F.3d 184 (5th Cir. 1995), the court of appeals confirmed that "the key inquiry in a book removal case is the school officials' substantial motivation in arriving at the removal decision." *Id.* at 190. Considering the plaintiffs' constitutional challenge to a school board's decision to remove a book on voodoo from the town's school libraries, the court held that a determination of the board's motivation could not be made without a trial. The court observed that "in light of the special role of the school library as a place where students may freely and voluntarily explore diverse topics, the School Board's non-curricular decision to remove a book well after it had been placed in the public school libraries evokes the question whether that action might not be an unconstitutional attempt to 'strangle the free mind at its source.'" *Id.*

Similarly, the district court in *Case v. Unified School District No. 233,* 908 F. Supp. 864 (D. Kan. 1995), found a school board's removal of *Annie on My Mind* unconstitutional where a "substantial motivation" behind the library removal was the officials' disagreement with the views expressed in the book. The defendants had claimed that the book was "educationally unsuitable," a removal criterion deemed permissible by the Supreme Court's plurality decision in *Pico. Pico,* 457 U.S. at 871. Nonetheless, the court refused to credit the defendant's assertions, explaining that "there is no basis in the record to believe that these Board members meant by 'educational suitability' anything other than their own disagreement with the ideas expressed in the book." *Case,* 908 F. Supp. at 875.

In a case that predates *Pico*, the court in *Minarcini v. Strongsville City School District*, 541 F.2d 577 (6th Cir. 1976), held that the First Amendment prohibited school officials from removing *Catch-22* and *Cat's Cradle* from the school library solely because the books conflicted with "the social or political tastes of the school board members." *Id.* at 582. Noting that "a library is a mighty resource in the free marketplace of ideas . . . specially dedicated to broad dissemination of ideas," *id.* at 582–83, the court distinguished the removal action from a decision not to approve or purchase certain texts, which the court found to be within the sound discretion of the school board.

More recently, a federal district court in Arkansas addressed a dispute over whether books from the Harry Potter series should be removed from a school library. A parent of two children in the Cedarville School District filed a complaint arguing that *Harry Potter and the Sorcerer's Stone* should be removed from the library. Following procedures for resolving challenges to library materials, the book was reviewed by the Library Committee. That committee of fifteen reviewers concluded unanimously that the book should remain in the library. The Cedarville School Board then ignored that decision and ordered that all of the books in the Harry Potter series be removed from the library shelves and held in the offices of the librarian for children with parental permission to read the books. *Counts v. Cedarville School District*, 295 F. Supp. 2d 996, 1000–01 (W.D. Ark. 2003).

Parents in the school district sued the school board, alleging that their child's rights were violated by the removal of the book from the open shelves of the library. The district court agreed. The court held that the minor's rights were violated even by the removal of the books from the open shelves because the books were "stigmatized." *Id.* at 999. The court held, moreover, that having to request the books from a librarian placed a burden on the minor's exercise of her First Amendment rights. The court also held that it was irrelevant that the minor plaintiff had the books at home, had parental permission, or otherwise had access to the books, because it violated her rights to remove it from the open shelves of her school library—absent a showing that the books were educationally unsuitable or pervasively vulgar. Finally, the court held that the school board did not allege a sufficient justification for the removal of the book in that there was no evidence to support the claim that the books would promote disobedience, disrespect for authority, or disruption in the school.

Overall, courts carefully scrutinize any decision to remove a book from a school library, imposing stricter constitutional standards than those applicable to curricular decisions. Certainly, the case law forbids any removal action motivated by the school officials' disagreement with the views or ideas expressed in the book. Even purportedly viewpoint-neutral justifications—such as "educational suitability"—likely will be subjected to skeptical, exacting judicial review.

Minors and the Internet

In a case considering a challenge to the Children's Internet Protection Act (CIPA), the Supreme Court plainly upheld the constitutionality of a filtering software system applicable to minors. *United States v. American Library Association,* 539 U.S. 194 (2003). Importantly, however, the Court recognized that the filtering must be disabled at the request of an adult and that minors also have a right to request unblocking of material constitutionally protected as to them.

CIPA provides that schools and libraries applying for certain funds for Internet access available pursuant to the Communications Act of 1934 (e-rate discounts) or the Museum and Library Services Act (LSTA grants) may not receive such funds unless they certify that they have in place a policy of Internet safety that includes the use of technology protection measures, that is, filtering or blocking software, that protects against access to certain visual depictions accessible through the Internet. Specifically, the school or library seeking funds must certify that it has filtering or blocking software in place that will block access for *minors* to visual depictions that are obscene, child pornography, or harmful to minors. The school or library must also certify that it has filtering or blocking software in place that will block access for *adults* to visual depictions that are obscene or child pornography. The technology protection measure must be placed on *all* computers, including those computers used by staff. An administrator, supervisor, or other authorized person may disable the filtering software for adults, but only to enable access for "bona fide research or other lawful purposes."[3]

CIPA was challenged in two lawsuits filed in the Eastern District of Pennsylvania. Both lawsuits alleged that application of CIPA in the context of the public library violated the First Amendment. On May 31, 2002, a three-judge panel held unanimously that the statute was unconstitutional. The court's holding was premised on the finding that "because of the inherent limitations in filtering technology, public libraries can never comply with CIPA without blocking access to a substantial amount of speech that is both constitutionally protected and fails to meet even the filtering companies' own blocking criteria." *American Library Association v. United States,* 201 F. Supp. 2d 401, 453 (E.D. Pa. 2002). The court also concluded that the disabling provision did not cure the unconstitutionality of the statute, because requiring a patron to request access to constitutionally protected speech was stigmatizing and significantly burdened the patron's First Amendment rights.

In June 2003, the Supreme Court reversed the holding of the court below in a plurality opinion. The reversal was premised on the fact that six of the nine justices of the Supreme Court accepted the solicitor general's assurance during oral argument that adults could request that filtering be disabled without specifying any reason for the disabling request. Thus, in the plurality opinion, Chief Justice Rehnquist (joined by Justices O'Connor, Scalia, and Thomas) concluded that the statute was not unconstitutional because "the Solicitor General confirmed that a 'librarian can, in response to a request from a patron, unblock the filtering mechanism altogether' . . . and further explained that a patron would not 'have to explain . . . why he was asking a site to be unblocked or the filtering to be disabled.'" *United States v. American Library Association,* 539 U.S. at 209.

The Court's plurality opinion contemplated that "when a patron encounters a blocked site, he need only ask a librarian to unblock it or (at least in the case of adults) disable the filter." *Id.* at 2306. Thus, although it would appear to be impermissible for a librarian to disable the filter entirely for a minor, librarians may unblock particular sites for minors. And, in fact, given that minors have explicit First Amendment rights, it would raise serious constitutional questions if a librarian refused to unblock a site that did not constitute obscenity, child pornography, or material harmful to minors.

Conclusion

It is well established that minors have First Amendment rights and that the constitutional right includes the right to receive information. Although school officials retain substantial discretion in designing school curricula, attempts to censor access to materials in the school library and public library will not be permitted absent a demonstration that the restricted materials are educationally unsuitable or pervasively vulgar. Although the Supreme Court has permitted the federal government in CIPA to require the use of filtering systems on public library terminals, the Court nonetheless recognized that both adults and minors have the right to access material that is constitutionally protected.

NOTES

1. Other cases in which the Supreme Court emphasized minors' right to receive information include *Erznoznik v. City of Jacksonville,* 422 U.S. 205, 213–14 (1975) (holding that "speech . . . cannot be suppressed solely to protect the young from ideas or images that a legislative body thinks unsuitable for them") and *Bolger v. Youngs Drug Products Corp.,* 463 U.S. 60, 75 n.30 (1983) (criticizing a federal ban on mailing unsolicited contraceptive advertisements because it ignored adolescents' "pressing need for information about contraception").
2. See also, e.g., *Virgil,* 862 F.2d at 1520–21 and n.3 (citing cases rejecting First Amendment claims that challenged various curricular decisions).
3. These statues are codified at 20 U.S.C. § 9134(f)(3) and 47 U.S.C. § 254(h)(6)(D).

Workbook for Selection Policy Writing

Office for Intellectual Freedom, American Library Association

Why Do I Need a Policy?

Every school system should have a comprehensive policy on the selection of instructional materials. It should relate to and include all materials; for example, textbooks, library books and materials, and all supplementary resources. The reason should be obvious: haphazard patterns of acquisition will result in waste because some—perhaps many—materials will overlap in content, or will be unrelated to changing patterns of instruction.

A comprehensive policy on the selection of instructional materials also will enable school professionals to rationally explain the school program to the community. And, most important in a crisis, when there are complaints about social studies texts, human development materials in the media center, or required reading in the English class, the use of the "objectionable" item can be explained more easily.

A good policy on the selection of instructional materials will be relevant to your particular system and include basic sections on objectives, responsibility, criteria, procedures for selection, reconsideration of materials, and policies on controversial materials.

Basic Components of a Selection Policy

OBJECTIVES

Your policy should state succinctly what your system is trying to accomplish in its educational program, and, in somewhat more detail, the objectives of selection.

Your overarching goal may be very broad. For example:

For the School District

- Instructional materials are selected by the school district to implement, enrich, and support the educational program for the student. Materials must serve both the breadth of the curriculum and the needs and interests of individual students. The district is obligated to provide for a wide range of abilities and to respect the diversity of many differing points of view. To this end, principles must be placed above personal opinion and reason above prejudice in the selection of materials of the highest quality and appropriateness.

For the Library Media Center

- The main objective of our selection procedure is to provide students with a wide range of educational materials on all levels of difficulty and in a variety of formats, with diversity of appeal, allowing for the presentation of many different points of view.
- The objective of the media center is to make available to faculty and students a collection of materials that will enrich and support the curriculum and meet the needs of the students and faculty served.

More specific goals should be established by professionals for each learning level.

The objectives for selection should reflect the specific goals of the instructional program. For textbooks, the goals may vary from subject to subject. For example, in the sciences, one principal goal might be accuracy (e.g., the latest scientific knowledge), and in history, balance in the presentation of conflicting points of view. For materials in the library media center, the goals may include meeting individual learning needs, abilities, and learning styles; providing background materials to supplement classroom instruction; providing a broad range of materials on controversial issues to help students develop critical analytical skills; etc.

RESPONSIBILITY FOR SELECTION

Your policy should name by professional position those persons responsible for selecting textbooks and other instructional materials.

In most states, the locally elected or appointed school board, by law, has broad powers and responsibilities in the selection of instructional materials. This authority should be delegated by policy to appropriate professionals for day-to-day exercise.

While selection of materials involves many people, including administrators, supervisors, teachers, library media specialists, students, and even community residents, the responsibility for coordinating and recommending the selection and purchase of library media materials should rest with the certified library media personnel. Responsibility for coordinating the selection and purchase of textbooks and other classroom materials may

rest with appropriate department chairpersons or with textbook or media evaluation committees.

Write into your policy under "Responsibility for Selection" (or similar title) exactly who is responsible for selection of materials; for example, department heads, curriculum specialists, directors of curriculum and instruction, librarians, or media specialists.

Sample Statement of Responsibility for the School District

The elected Board of Education shall delegate to the Superintendent of Schools the authority and responsibility for selection of all print and non-print materials. Responsibilities for actual selection shall rest with appropriate professionally trained personnel who shall discharge this obligation consistent with the Board's adopted selection criteria and procedures. Selection procedures shall involve representatives of the professional staff directly affected by the selections, and persons qualified by preparation to aid in wise selection.

CRITERIA

For the subject matter covered, your policy will include criteria, and the application of criteria, relevant to your objectives: excellence (artistic, literary, etc.), appropriateness to level of user, superiority in treatment of controversial issues, and ability to stimulate further intellectual and social development.

Consider authenticity, appropriateness, interest, content, and circumstances of use.

You probably will want to include technical criteria in your policy; for example, clarity of sound in audio materials and cinematography in films.

Specific criteria should be spelled out to guide all professionals involved in selection in deciding on specific items:

Staff members involved in selection of resource materials shall use the following criteria as a guide:

- educational significance
- contribution the subject matter makes to the curriculum and to the interests of the students
- favorable reviews found in standard selection sources
- favorable recommendations based on preview and examination of materials by professional personnel
- reputation and significance of the author, producer, and publisher
- validity, currency, and appropriateness of material
- contribution the material makes to breadth of representative viewpoints on controversial issues
- high degree of potential user appeal
- high artistic quality and/or literary style
- quality and variety of format
- value commensurate with cost and/or need

- timeliness or permanence
- integrity

The following recommended lists shall be consulted in the selection of materials, but selection is not limited to their listings:

Bibliographies (latest editions available, including supplements), such as

- *Children's Catalog*
- *Middle and Junior High Core Collection*
- *Senior High Core Collection*
- *Nonbook Materials Core Collection*
- *Subject Guide to Children's Books in Print*
- ALSC Notable Children's Books
- YALSA Best Books for Young Adults
- Notable Social Studies Trade Books K–12
- Outstanding Science Trade Books K–12

Current reviewing media

- *AASA Science Books and Films Online*
- *Booklist*
- *Book Links*
- *Bulletin of the Center for Children's Books*
- *Horn Book*

- *Kirkus Reviews*
- *Library Journal*
- *School Library Journal*

The following criteria will be used as they apply:

1. Learning resources shall support and be consistent with the general educational goals of the state and district and the aims and objectives of individual schools and specific courses.
2. Learning resources shall meet high standards of quality in factual content and presentation.
3. Learning resources shall be appropriate for the subject area and for the age, emotional development, ability level, learning styles, and social development of the students for whom the materials are selected.
4. Physical format and appearance of learning resources shall be suitable for their intended use.
5. Learning resources shall be designed to help students gain an awareness of our pluralistic society.
6. Learning resources shall be designed to motivate students and staff to examine their own duties, responsibilities, rights, and privileges as participating citizens in our society, and to make informed judgments in their daily lives.
7. Learning resources shall be selected for their strengths rather than rejected for their weaknesses.

8. The selection of learning resources on controversial issues will be directed toward maintaining a diverse collection representing various views.
9. Learning resources shall clarify historical and contemporary forces by presenting and analyzing intergroup tension and conflict objectively, placing emphasis on recognizing and understanding social and economic problems.

The following kinds of material should be selected for the media center:

1. Materials integral to the instructional program.
2. Materials appropriate for the reading level and understanding of students in the school.
3. Materials reflecting the interests and needs of the students and faculty served by the media center.
4. Materials warranting inclusion in the collection because of their literary and/or artistic value and merit.
5. Materials presenting information with the greatest degree of accuracy and clarity possible.
6. Materials representing a fair and unbiased presentation of information. In controversial areas, the media specialist, in cooperation with the faculty, should select materials representing as many shades of opinion as possible, in order that varying viewpoints are available to students.

PROCEDURES

Your procedures should describe all steps from initial screening to final selection. They also should include provisions for coordinating among departments and professionals working at different learning levels, etc.; for handling recommendations from other faculty and students and for reviewing existing materials (for possible replacement, etc.).

Include at least a partial list of selection aids (e.g., reviewing sources). You also may want to list sources that should not be used.

This will be a large part of your selection policy. It is important to list the types of materials you collect, why you need them, and how you obtain them. Include here your policies on reevaluation (weeding), replacing and repairing materials, etc.

Sample Procedure Statements

1. In selecting learning resources, professional personnel will evaluate available resources and curriculum needs and will consult reputable, professionally prepared aids to selection, and other appropriate sources. The actual resource will be examined whenever possible.

2. Recommendations for purchase involve administrators, teachers, students, district personnel, and community persons, as appropriate.

3. Gift materials shall be judged by the selection criteria and shall be accepted or rejected by those criteria.

4. Selection is an ongoing process that should include how to remove materials no longer appropriate and how to replace lost and worn materials still of educational value.

5. Requests, suggestions, and reactions for the purchase of instructional materials shall be gathered from staff to the greatest extent possible and from students when appropriate.

6. Reviews of proposed acquisitions will be sought in the literature of reputable professional organizations and other reviewing sources recognized for their objectivity and wide experience.

7. Materials will be examined by professional staff to the extent necessary or practicable to apply criteria. Preview copies are available for on-site examination by the public upon written request to the District Director of Instruction.

8. Textbooks will be selected after examination by a representative committee of teachers, principals, curriculum specialists, directors of instruction, and others who have professional expertise in objective evaluation of materials.

9. Materials for the District Film Center will be selected by preview committees, curriculum specialists, and through use of professional review sources.

10. Building media center materials selection will be coordinated by the building media specialist, or the principal, where there is no professional staff, and involve teachers and curriculum specialists.
11. Area Advisory Councils may be used to review materials recommended by professional selection committees.
12. Materials for media centers are selected by the professional media staff with due regard to suggestions from the faculty, parents, and students. Final selection is made by the media specialists of the school in which the center is housed. Professionally recognized reviewing periodicals, standard catalogs, and other selection aids are used by the media specialists and the faculty to guide them in their selection.

SPECIAL AREAS

Some miscellaneous items to consider in your policy are gifts, sponsored materials, expensive materials, ephemeral materials, jobbers and salespersons, locked case, special requests, etc.; free and inexpensive materials; professional materials; and procedure for handling lost materials. Do you charge fines, maintain special collections not available to all patrons (e.g., a collection of materials for teachers only), handle special requests? These "special concerns" can be detailed in this section of your policy. Make sure to include your procedures for integrating gifts and sponsored materials. Usually, it is stated that criteria for inclusion of gifts and sponsored materials are the same as for purchased materials.

POLICIES ON CONTROVERSIAL MATERIALS

Here, or in another place in your policy, you should include a statement on intellectual freedom and why it is important to maintain. You may wish to include the text of the First Amendment to the United States Constitution—"Congress shall make no law respecting an establishment of religion, or prohibiting the free exercise thereof; or abridging the freedom of speech, or of the press; or the right of the people peaceable to assemble, and to petition the Government for a redress of grievances," and the *Library Bill of Rights* [a copy is included at the beginning of this book].

Sample Statement on Intellectual Freedom

> The school board subscribes in principle to the statements of policy on library philosophy as expressed in the American Library Association's *Library Bill of Rights,* a copy of which is appended to and made a part of this policy.

RECONSIDERATION

Occasional objections to instructional materials will be made despite the quality of the selection process; therefore, the procedure for handling reconsideration of challenged materials in response to questions concerning their appropriateness should be stated. This procedure should establish the framework for registering a complaint that provides for a hearing with appropriate action while defending the principles of freedom of information, the students' right to access of materials, and the professional responsibility and integrity of the school faculty. The principles of intellectual freedom are inherent in the First Amendment to the Constitution of the United States and are expressed in the *Library Bill of Rights,* adopted by the Council of the American Library Association. If instructional materials are questioned, the principles of intellectual freedom should be defended rather than the materials.

List here the specific steps that will be taken when you are asked to reconsider materials in your collection. These steps should include

- asking the complainant to fill out a written complaint form. (See Sample Request for Reconsideration of Library Resources.)
- assigning a reconsideration committee to examine the materials in question.
- requesting that the committee report their findings to the school board.

The procedure for handling complaints should describe every step, from the initial response to the complaint through the highest appeal.

Procedures for Handling Complaints

No duly selected materials whose appropriateness is challenged shall be removed from the school except upon the recommendation of a reconsideration committee, with the concurrence of the Superintendent or, upon the Superintendent's recommendation, the concurrence of the Board of Education, or upon formal action of the Board of Education when a recommendation of a reconsideration committee is appealed to it.

Procedures to be observed

- All complaints to staff members shall be reported to the building principal involved, whether received by telephone, letter, or in personal conversation.
- The principal shall contact the complainant to discuss the complaint and attempt to resolve it informally by explaining the philosophy and goals of the school district and/or the library media center.
- If the complaint is not resolved informally, the complainant shall be supplied with a packet of materials consisting of the District's instructional goals and objectives, materials selection policy statement, and the procedure for handling objections. This packet also will include a standard printed form, which shall be completed and returned before consideration will be given to the complaint.

- If the formal request for reconsideration has not been received by the principal within two weeks, it shall be considered closed. If the request is returned, the reasons for selection of the specific work shall be reestablished by the appropriate staff.
- In accordance with statement of philosophy, no questioned materials shall be removed from the school pending a final decision. Pending the outcome of the request for reconsideration, however, access to questioned materials can be denied to the child (or children) of the parents making the complaint, if they so desire.
- Upon receipt of a completed objection form, the principal in the building involved will convene a committee of five to consider the complaint. This committee shall consist of the curriculum director and these people from the school involved: the principal, the library media center director, a teacher, and a PTA representative.
- The committee shall meet to discuss the materials, following the guidelines set forth in Instructions to Reconsideration Committee, and shall prepare a report on the material containing its recommendations on disposition of the matter.
- The principal shall notify complainant of the decision and send a formal report and recommendation to the Superintendent. In answering the complainant, the principal shall explain the book selection system, give the guidelines used for selection, and cite authorities used in reaching decisions. If the committee decides to keep the work that caused the complaint, the complainant shall be given an explanation. If the complaint is valid, the principal will acknowledge it and make recommended changes.
- If the complainant is still not satisfied, he or she may ask the Superintendent to present an appeal to the Board of Education, which shall make a final determination of the issue. The Board of Education may seek assistance from outside organizations such as the American Library Association, the Association for Supervision and Curriculum Development, etc., in making its determination.

Sample Letter to Complainant

Dear _____:

We appreciate your concern over the use of _____
_____ in our school district. The district
has developed procedures for selecting materials, but realizes that not everyone will
agree with every selection made.

    To help you understand the selection process, we are sending copies of the
district's

1.   Instructional goals and objectives
2.   Materials Selection Policy statement
3.   Procedure for Handling Objections

    If you are still concerned after you review this material, please complete the
Request for Reconsideration of Material form and return it to me. You may be assured
of prompt attention to your request. If I have not heard from you within two weeks,
we will assume you no longer wish to file a formal complaint.

Sincerely,

_____
Principal

Instructions to Reconsideration Committee

Bear in mind the principles of the freedom to learn and to read and base your decision on these broad principles rather than on defense of individual materials. Freedom of inquiry is vital to education in a democracy.

Study thoroughly all materials referred to you and read available reviews. The general acceptance of the materials should be checked by consulting standard evaluation aids and local holdings in other schools.

Passages or parts should not be pulled out of context. The values and faults should be weighed against each other and the opinions based on the materials as a whole.

Your report, presenting both majority and minority opinions, will be presented by the principal to the complainant at the conclusion of your discussion of the questioned material.

Sample Request for Reconsideration of Library Resources

[This is where you identify who in your own structure has authorized use of this form—Director, Board of Trustees, Board of Education, etc.—and to whom to return the form. See the example below.]

The school board of Mainstream County, U.S.A., has delegated the responsibility for selection and evaluation of library/educational resources to the school library media specialist/curriculum committee, and has established reconsideration procedures to address concerns about those resources. Completion of this form is the first step in those procedures. If you wish to request reconsideration of school or library resources, please return the completed form to the Coordinator of Library Media Resources, Mainstream School Dist., 1 Mainstream Plaza, Anytown, U.S.A.

Name _____ Date _____

Address _____ City _____ State _____

Zip _____ Phone _____

Do you represent self? _____ Organization? _____

1. Resource on which you are commenting:

   _____ Book _____ Textbook _____ Video _____ Display _____ Magazine _____ Library Program _____ Audio Recording
   _____ Newspaper _____ Electronic Information/Network (please specify): _____
   _____ Other _____

   Title _____ Author/Producer _____

2. What brought this resource to your attention? _____
_____
_____

3. Have you examined the entire resource? _____

4. What concerns you about the resource? (use other side or additional pages if necessary) _____
_____
_____

5. Are there resource(s) you suggest to provide additional information and/or other viewpoints on this topic? _____
_____
_____

Revised by the American Library Association Intellectual Freedom Committee, June 27, 1995.

Sample Selection Policy

Selection Policy
School District #1

PART 1: SELECTION OF LEARNING RESOURCES

I. Statement of Policy

The policy of the Board of Trustees of School District #1 is to provide a wide range of learning resources at varying levels of difficulty, with diversity of appeal and the presentation of different points of view to meet the needs of students and teachers.

II. Objectives of Selection

For the purposes of this statement of policy, the term "learning resources" will refer to any person(s) or any material (whether acquired or locally produced) with instructional content or function that is used for formal or informal teaching/learning purposes. Learning resources include textbooks, other books, charts, maps and globes, models and realia, pictures, games, data files, websites, motion pictures and DVDs, periodicals and monographs, slides, sound recordings, printed music, and transparencies. Community people, agencies and organizations are vital "learning resources," as well as national and international agencies, museums, libraries and other educational institutions that offer programs via the Internet or satellite.

A. The primary objective of learning resources is to support, enrich, and help implement the educational program of the school through the interaction of professional personnel and other members of the school community. It is the duty of professional staff to provide students with a wide range of materials at varying levels of difficulty, with diversity of appeal, and the presentation of different points of view.

B. To this end, the Board of Trustees of School District #1 affirms that it is the responsibility of its professional staff:

1. To provide materials that will enrich and support the curriculum, taking into consideration the varied interests, abilities, learning styles, and maturity levels of the students served;

2. To provide materials that will stimulate growth in factual knowledge, literary appreciation, aesthetic values, and societal standards;

3. To provide materials on various sides of controversial issues so that young citizens may

have an opportunity to develop under guidance the practice of critical analysis and to make informed judgments in their daily lives;

4. To provide materials representative of the many religious, ethnic, and cultural groups and that contribute to our national heritage and the world community;

5. To place principle above personal opinion and reason above prejudice in the selection of materials of the highest quality in order to assure a comprehensive collection appropriate to the school community.

III. Responsibility for Selection of Learning Resources

A. The Board of Trustees delegates the responsibility for the selection of learning resources to the professional staff employed by the school system, and declares that selections made shall be held to have been made by the Board of Trustees of School District #1.

B. While selection of learning resources involves many people (administrators, teachers, students, community persons, resource center personnel) the responsibility for coordinating the selection of school learning resources and making the recommendation

for purchase rests with the principal and professional personnel.

IV. Criteria for Selection of Learning Resources

A. The following criteria will be used as they apply:

1. Learning resources shall support and be consistent with the general educational goals of the state and the district and the aims and objectives of individual schools and specific courses.

2. Learning resources shall be chosen to enrich and support the curriculum and the personal needs of users.

3. Learning resources shall meet high standards of quality in
   - artistic quality and/or literary style
   - authenticity
   - educational significance
   - factual content
   - physical format
   - presentation
   - readability
   - technical quality

4. Learning resources shall be appropriate for the subject area and for the age, emotional

development, ability level, learning styles, and social development of the students for whom the materials are selected.

5. Learning resources shall be designed to provide a background of information that will motivate students and staff to examine their own attitudes and behavior; to comprehend their duties, responsibilities, rights and privileges as participating citizens in our society; and to make informed judgments in their daily lives.

6. Learning resources shall provide information on opposing sides of controversial issues so that users may develop under guidance the practice of critical analysis.

B. The selection of learning resources on controversial issues will be directed toward maintaining a balanced collection representing various views. Learning resources shall clarify historical and contemporary forces by presenting and analyzing intergroup tension and conflict objectively, placing emphasis on recognizing and understanding social and economic problems.

V. Procedures for Selection of Learning Resources

A. In selecting learning resources, professional personnel will evaluate available resources and curriculum needs and will consult reputable, professionally prepared aids to selection and other appropriate sources. Among sources to be consulted are

1. Bibliographies (latest edition available, including supplements), such as
   - *Children's Catalog*
   - *Middle and Junior High Core Collection*
   - *Senior High Core Collection*
   - *Nonbook Materials Core Collection*
2. Current reviewing media:
   - *AASA Science Books and Films OnLine*
   - *Bulletin of the Center for Children's Books*
   - *Horn Book*
   - *Kirkus Reviews*
   - *Booklist*
   - *Book Links*
   - *Library Journal*
   - *School Library Journal*
   - Other sources will be consulted as appropriate. Whenever possible, the actual resource will be examined.

B. Recommendations for purchase involve administrators, teachers, students, district personnel, and community persons, as appropriate.

C. Gift materials shall be judged by the criteria outlined and shall be accepted or rejected by those criteria.

D. Selection is an ongoing process that should include the removal of materials no longer appropriate and the replacement of lost and worn materials still of educational value.

PART 2: PROCEDURES FOR DEALING WITH CHALLENGED MATERIALS

I. Statement of Policy

Any resident or employee of the school district may formally challenge learning resources used in the district's educational program on the basis of appropriateness. This procedure is for the purpose of considering the opinions of those persons in the schools and the community who are not directly involved in the selection process.

II. Request for Informal Reconsideration

A. The school receiving a complaint regarding a learning resource shall try to resolve the issue informally.

1. The principal or other appropriate staff shall explain to the questioner the school's selection procedure, criteria, and qualifications of those persons selecting the resource.

2. The principal or other appropriate staff shall explain the particular place the questioned resource occupies in the education program, its intended educational usefulness, and additional information regarding its use, or refer the party to someone who can identify and explain the use of the resource.

3. If the questioner wishes to file a formal challenge, a copy of the district Selection of Learning Resources policy and a Request for Reconsideration of Learning Resources form shall be handed or mailed to the party concerned by the principal.

III. Request for Formal Reconsideration

A. Preliminary Procedures

1. Each school will keep on hand and make available Request for Reconsideration of Learning Resources forms. All formal objections to learning resources must be made on these forms.

2. The Request for Reconsideration of Learning Resources form shall be signed by the questioner

and filed with the principal or someone so designated by the principal.

3. The area assistant superintendent and the assistant superintendent of curriculum services shall be informed of the formal complaint received.

4. The request for reconsideration shall be referred to a reconsideration committee at the school level for reevaluation of the resource.

5. Requests for reconsideration of materials in district collections shall be referred to the school resource center consultative committee for reevaluation of the resource. This committee may involve additional personnel as appropriate.

B. The Reconsideration Committee

1. Upon receipt of a request for formal reconsideration of a learning resource, the principal shall

   a. Appoint a reconsideration committee including the following membership as appropriate:
      - One member of the district staff chosen by the area assistant superintendent;
      - One member of the school teaching staff chosen by the school staff;
      - One member of the resource center professional staff chosen by the resource center professional staff;
      - One member of the school consultative committee chosen by the school consultative committee;
      - Two students chosen by the student body.

   b. Name a convener of the reconsideration committee.

   c. Arrange for a reconsideration committee meeting within 10 working days after the complaint is received.

2. The reconsideration committee may choose to consult district support staff and/or community persons with related professional knowledge.

3. The reconsideration committee shall review the challenged resource and judge whether it conforms to the principles of selection outlined in the district's Selection of Learning Resources policy.

C. Resolution

1. The reconsideration committee shall

a. Examine the challenged resource;

b. Determine professional acceptance by reading critical reviews of the resource;

c. Weigh values and faults and form opinions based on the material as a whole rather than on passages or sections taken out of context;

d. Discuss the challenged resource in the context of the educational program;

e. Discuss the challenged item with the individual questioner when appropriate;

f. Prepare a written report.

2. The written report shall be discussed with the individual questioner if requested.

3. The written report shall be retained by the school principal, with copies forwarded to the assistant superintendent of curriculum services and the area assistant superintendent. A minority report also may be filed.

4. Written reports, once filed, are confidential and available for examination by trustees and appropriate officials only.

5. The decision of the reconsideration committee is binding for the individual school.

6. Notwithstanding any procedure outlined in this policy, the questioner shall have the right to appeal any decision of the reconsideration committee to the Board of Trustees as the final review panel.

D. Guiding Principles

1. Any resident or employee of the school district may raise objection to learning resources used in a school's educational program, despite the fact that the individuals selecting such resources were duly qualified to make the selection, followed the proper procedure, and observed the criteria for selecting learning resources.

2. The principal should review the selection and objection rules with the teaching staff at least annually. The staff should be reminded that the right to object to learning resources is one granted by policies enacted by the Board of Trustees.

3. No parent has the right to determine reading, viewing, or listening matter for students other than his or her own children.

4. School District #1 supports the *Library Bill of Rights,* adopted by the American Library

Association. (A copy of the *Library Bill of Rights* is attached to this policy.) When learning resources are challenged, the principles of the freedom to read/listen/view must be defended as well.

5. Access to challenged material shall not be restricted during the reconsideration process.
6. The major criterion for the final decision is the appropriateness of the material for its intended educational use.
7. A decision to sustain a challenge shall not necessarily be interpreted as a judgment of irresponsibility by the professionals involved in the original selection or use of the material.

Revised October 1999

ADDITIONAL RESOURCES

Censorship and Challenges: www.ala.org/ala/aboutala/offices/oif/basics/intellectual.cfm

Coping with Challenges: Kids and Libraries: www.ala.org/ala/aboutala/offices/oif/challengesupport/dealing/copingchallenges.cfm

Coping with Challenges: Strategies and Tips for Dealing with Challenges to Library Materials: www.ala.org/ala/aboutala/offices/oif/challengesupport/dealing/copingchallengesstrategies.cfm

Freedom to Read statement: www.ala.org/ala/aboutala/offices/oif/statementspols/ftrstatement/freedomreadstatement.cfm

Library Bill of Rights: www.ala.org/ala/aboutala/offices/oif/statementspols/statementsif/librarybillrights.cfm

Reporting a Challenge: www.ala.org/ala/aboutala/offices/oif/challengesupport/reporting/reportingchallenge.cfm

Index

selection criteria *(cont.)*
 sample goals, 8
 in selection policy, 125–127, 136–137
selection tools, 4, 126–127
self-censorship and collection management, 36
sex education materials and restrictions, 57
shelving of beginning reader materials, 38. *See also* restricted materials
social networking, 107–108
social security numbers, privacy of, 73
Spanish-language materials, 15–16
special needs, students with, 60–61, 79. *See also* disabled students
state history assignments and interlibrary loan, 41, 43
student newspapers, 115
student websites, 105–106
students
 freedom of speech rights of, 111–112
 individual needs of, 15–16
 instructions on privacy, 89, 90
 responses to challenges, 53
 responsibility for Internet use, 103–105, 106
 setting of behavior standards by, 67, 69
 setting of Internet guidelines by, 108
subpoenas for library records, 84

T

Technology, Education, and Copyright Harmonization (TEACH) Act (2002), 46
testing and closures of library, 64

time management and student privacy, 81
Tinker v. Des Moines Indep. Community Sch. Dist., 29, 111

U

unacceptable uses of Internet, 99
unblocking websites, 100–101, 120–121. *See also* filtering
United States v. American Library Association, 119
United States v. Friedman, 30
USA PATRIOT Act, 84–85

V

vandalism
 in Internet acceptable-use policy, 99
 statutes governing, 7
Virgil v. School Bd. of Columbia County, 116
viruses, computer, 99

W

websites, log-in records for, 86
West Virginia State Bd. of Educ. v. Barnette, 30

You may also be interested in

Intellectual Freedom Manual, Seventh Edition:
The seventh edition includes the most up-to-date intellectual freedom guidelines, policies, and interpretations of the Library Bill of Rights, along with the ALA Code of Ethics and Freedom to Read Statement.

The Whole School Library Handbook: Modeled on the format of ALA's bestselling *Whole Library Handbook* (1998), this book is the one-stop resource for everything related to the school library media center. Inside this handy reference, you'll find essential facts, thought-provoking articles, checklists, organization contact information, trivia, advice from the field's experts, and much more!

Collaborative Strategies for Teaching Reading Comprehension: Time-strapped educators wonder whether partnering with teacher-librarians will realistically improve students' scores. Drawing on cutting-edge research in instructional strategies, Judi Moreillon, a veteran teacher-librarian, offers a clear, rigorous roadmap to the task of teaching reading comprehension in a proven collaborative process. In the national drive to improve test scores and build a nation of readers, the strategies included are proven teamwork tools to accomplish both goals.

Hit List for Children 2: *Harry Potter and the Sorcerer's Stone, A Wrinkle in Time, Blubber, Scary Stories to Tell in the Dark*—these are some of the most beloved, and most challenged, books for children. Leaving controversial titles such as these out of your collection or limiting their access is not the answer to challenges. The best-selling *Hit List* series gives you the information you need to defend challenged books with an informed response, all the while ensuring free access to young book lovers.

Check out these and other great titles at www.alastore.ala.org!